the tipping points
from doubt to faith

GOD IN PURSUIT

joseph bentz

D1559167

BEACON HILL PRESS
OF KANSAS CITY

Library of Congress Cataloging-in-Publication Data

Bentz, Joseph, 1961-
   God in pursuit : the tipping points from doubt to faith / Joseph Bentz.
      p. cm.
   Includes bibliographpical references (p.   ).
   ISBN 978-0-8341-2492-9 (pbk.)
   1. Conversion—Christianity. I. Title.
   BV4916.3.B46 2010
   248.2'4—dc22

                                                              2009039742

10 9 8 7 6 5 4 3 2 1

Contents

Introduction   5

1. "I Didn't Want to Be a Christian, but . . ."
   The Pursuing God   11

2. Awakened: Light and Foreshadow   27

3. Breaking Through to Faith: The Meaning of Conversion   44

4. Tipping Point 1: When God Finds You at Your Lowest Point   53

5. Tipping Point 2:
   When Circumstances and a Spiritual Messenger Conspire   65

6. Tipping Point 3: When the Convicting Need for Spiritual
   Transformation Won't Let You Go   79

7. Tipping Point 4: When the Word Speaks with
   Undeniable Clarity and Power   89

8. Tipping Point 5: When a Long Intellectual and
   Spiritual Persuasion Pushes You Toward Christ   99

9. Slightly Beyond the Tipping Point: Attacks of Doubt,
   the Impulse to Serve   113

10. Far Beyond the Tipping Point: The Dance of Doubt
    and Faith   125

11. Where Doubt May Lead: A Small Complaint
    About Suffering   136

Notes   153

Acknowledgments   158

About the Author   160

Contents

Introduction   5

1. "I Didn't Want to Be a Christian, but . . ."
   The Pursuing God   11

2. Awakened: Light and Foreshadow   27

3. Breaking Through to Faith: The Meaning of Conversion   44

4. Tipping Point 1: When God Finds You at Your Lowest Point   53

5. Tipping Point 2:
   When Circumstances and a Spiritual Messenger Conspire   65

6. Tipping Point 3: When the Convicting Need for Spiritual
   Transformation Won't Let You Go   79

7. Tipping Point 4: When the Word Speaks with
   Undeniable Clarity and Power   89

8. Tipping Point 5: When a Long Intellectual and
   Spiritual Persuasion Pushes You Toward Christ   99

9. Slightly Beyond the Tipping Point: Attacks of Doubt,
   the Impulse to Serve   113

10. Far Beyond the Tipping Point: The Dance of Doubt
    and Faith   125

11. Where Doubt May Lead: A Small Complaint
    About Suffering   136

Notes   153

Acknowledgments   158

About the Author   160

Introduction

We live in an age of disbelief and hostility to Christianity. Books by celebrity atheists regularly hit the bestseller lists. Groups offer ceremonies in which adults can be "de-baptized" and "de-converted." Atheists who feel threatened by a God they don't believe in buy advertisements on buses, billboards, and the radio to deny His existence. Parents send their children to atheist summer camps. Atheists have their own congressional lobbyist.

Yet in spite of attacks from every direction, God's disruptive Spirit keeps invading people's lives, drawing even the unlikeliest individuals into relationship with Jesus Christ. How on earth does this happen?

What is the turning point that causes a curious journalist and atheist named Sara Miles to walk into a church at age 46 and be converted to Christ the first time she takes Communion? What persuades Francis Collins, a lifelong atheist and head of one of the greatest scientific breakthroughs of the twentieth century, the Human Genome Project, to turn to Christ and become "a believer in a God who is unlimited by time and space, and who takes personal interest in human beings"?[1] What leads a woman like Mary Kay Beard, who had a Mafia contract on her life and appeared on the FBI's Ten Most Wanted list, to become a Christian in prison before starting the national Angel Tree ministry, which has touched the lives of untold thousands of children?

When I approached this book, I wanted to know, *What is that spark that allows faith to catch fire in the lives of new believers who were once hostile or indifferent to God?* Do most people follow a similar process, or are there as many tipping points from doubt to faith as there are people telling their stories? Once people make that leap of faith and become Christians, what happens throughout their lives as they hit crises of doubt or confusion or when they confront spiritual issues that may not have arisen at the time of conversion? Are the turning points from doubt to deeper faith—or from doubt to loss of faith—similar during crisis times as they are at the point of conversion?

I sought answers by studying dozens of conversion stories and by interviewing people about their own conversions. I studied conversions that happened during the last few years, conversions that happened thirty or forty years ago, conversions that occurred hundreds of years ago. I looked at the Puritan era. I looked at the Nixon era. I read compilations of conversion stories such as Hugh T. Kerr and John M. Mulder's fascinating book *Famous Conversions*, which compiles stories from Constantine to Charles Colson. I gathered accounts from strangers and from friends at church, and I even examined my own conversion. I studied the books of conversion experts like William James, Richard Peace, and Lewis Rambo.

What I found was inspiring. When I saw the enormous range of people God reaches and the wide variety of ways He reaches them, I was filled with hope for what He may still do in my own life and in the lives of people I love. This book is not a scientific study, and it is not a sociological or psychological analysis of conversion. It is a celebration of the ways people find God—and the ways He finds them—both at conversion and in periods of doubt during their Christian life. The book starts with some of the most resistant converts of all, people who were not just mildly skeptical of Christianity but who, in fact, had no intention of ever following Jesus Christ. Some of them knew they would pay a heavy price among family and friends if they followed Christ. Some risked livelihoods and their standing in the community. Some risked their very lives. But when Jesus showed up, they followed. Why?

The early chapters in this book examine two factors important in many conversions even before people reach the tipping point. One is "foreshadowing," the idea that even though a conversion to Christ may look sudden, it's usually preceded by clues—people, books, experiences, and other details—that have prepared that person for the day when God arrives.

Another element that kept surfacing as I learned people's stories is *"kairos,"* or "loaded time," a period separated from all the ordinary moments of life when a person is particularly awake to the presence of the Holy Spirit. The person may have heard the Christian message a thousand times, yet it never penetrated. But during this "loaded time," God seems particularly close, and the truth of the gospel burns in the person as never before. The existence of foreshadowing and loaded time indicates a God who pursues people, who is busy laying clues, preparing people to hear Him, loving them into His presence.

I read and listened to conversion stories not knowing what patterns or common tipping points, if any, would emerge. Even though the details of the stories were vastly different, they began falling into several recognizable patterns. Suffering intense physical or emotional crisis was one turning point I saw in many conversions. For these converts, such as influential politician Ninoy Aquino, who was tossed into prison naked and powerless, or John Newton, who faced almost certain death in a storm at sea, the crisis woke them up to what was really important in life. They were forced out of the misleading complacency in which many people spend their existence, and they searched for truth that would satisfy them for eternity.

Like other tipping points, suffering can tip people either way—toward God or farther away from Him. Circumstances that are a turning point for some people leave others unmoved. Some need what I call a spiritual messenger to lead them to Christ. I found amazing stories of people who were opened to the gospel by someone who entered their lives at just the right moment. Sometimes these were friends who carefully counseled the person, while at other times they were strangers who spoke a message that penetrated beyond what they could have known.

For some, a particular awareness of sin and the powerful conviction that only Jesus Christ can save them from it was the turning point. For others, the Bible, which they may never have read before or may have read as a child but neglected for decades, suddenly blazed forth with a clarity and truth they could not have imagined. Others, like C. S. Lewis or Malcolm Muggeridge, turned to God only after a long intellectual and spiritual struggle, once their old assumptions were rocked and the truth of Jesus Christ still remained inescapable.

Stepping into faith as a new Christian doesn't mean doubt is forever vanquished, of course. The Christian life is far too messy and much too dynamic for that. One thing I've noticed about most Christian conversions is that they happen in the *middle* of busy lives, when people are minding their own business, just trying to get by. They may turn to Him and become believers, but many questions remain unanswered at that moment of conversion. Some questions haven't even occurred to them yet, and others wouldn't yet be relevant to them even if they did come up.

Years after conversion, however, circumstances such as suffering or intellectual objections or spiritual burnout may push the believer to another tipping point of doubt or faith. Some turn away from their faith at this point, others try to ignore or deny the doubts, and yet others confront the doubts head-on and work through them until they arrive at an even deeper and more mature faith.

What Difference Does This Make?

Why should you care about the tipping points between doubt and faith? This book shows that God is monumentally *unsettling* in people's lives, not only at the time of conversion but also throughout the Christian journey. It's easy to think of doubt as an enemy to be crushed or avoided, but in fact, doubt and spiritual crisis are often necessary preludes to deeper belief. The greatest spiritual progress is often accompanied by the most doubt and bewilderment. In this sense the spiritual journey is similar to other areas of human experience such as the long periods of uncertainty and questioning a scientist goes through to reach a groundbreaking discovery. The researcher striving for a scientific breakthrough does not begin with answers. Instead, he or she begins with questions, with trial and error, with trepidation that the answer sought may never arise from the daunting array of possible solutions. The easiest thing to do would be to turn away from this confusion and simply stick to what he or she already knows. Instead, the scientist understands that the only path to the breakthrough is *through* the perplexity. There's no shortcut around it.

So it is with the non-believer who reaches the tipping point into faith or the Christian who faces doubt. The only path to the spiritual breakthrough is *through* the doubt. Denying it or explaining it away may offer temporary solace, but that path leads only to stagnation.

God shows up in people's lives in creative ways they could never predict and at times they would least expect. That "loaded time" in your own life may have arrived. Your own situation may be reflected in the stories of those in this book who reached the turning point into faith as new converts or as Christians in crisis.

If He can reach Paul in a flash of light, John Newton in a storm at sea, John Woolman in a life-threatening illness, and Mary Kay Beard through a prison Bible, how might He reach you? Will you be listening when He speaks? If you're interested in probing the influences that open the door into greater faith, then I invite you to read on.

ONE

"I Didn't Want to Be a Christian, but . . ."
The Pursuing God

Sara Miles did not want to be a Christian. Anne Lamott did not want to be a Christian. C. S. Lewis did not want to be a Christian. Neither did R. A. Torrey, Ziya Meral, Lin Yutang, Jim Vaus, or a dozen others I could name.

How do people find God when they're running away from Him as fast as they can? Those of us who have agonized over our spiritual journeys know it's hard to find Him when you're searching for Him with all your might—when you're praying, reading scripture, hearing sermons, seeking guidance from Christian friends and pastors. I've read of seekers throughout history who have spent days, months, even years reaching out to God and wrestling with doubts over their salvation. Some of them never do find complete assurance. So how much hope is there for those who simply don't want to be bothered with God? What about those who are actively hostile toward Him or who don't even believe He exists or who dislike Christians and Christianity so much that they would be horrified to think of themselves as having any association with such people?

Sara Miles was not fond of Christians. She describes herself as "a blue-state, secular intellectual; a lesbian, a left-wing journalist with a habit of skepticism." Although her grandparents were Christian missionaries, her parents rejected what they saw as "the whole unbelievable, illogical concept" of God, and they raised their daughter in an atheist home. Most of what she associated with Christianity—"ecstatic teen crusaders in suburban megachurches, slick preachers proclaiming the 'gospel' of prosperity, and shrewd political organizers who rail against evolution, gay marriage, and stem-cell research"—she loathed. What could Christianity possibly have to offer her? "I had no particular affection for this figure named 'Jesus,'" she writes, "no echo of childhood friendly feeling for the guy with the beard and the robes."[1] Why would she even consider turning her life upside down and facing the derision of her family and her entire social circle in order to embrace Him?

Anne Lamott does not sound like a good candidate for Christianity either. Like Sara Miles, she grew up in a household of atheists where belief in God was scorned. "None of the adults in our circle believed," wrote Lamott. "Believing meant that you were stupid. Ignorant people believed, uncouth people believed, and we were heavily couth."[2] As an adult, Lamott became a successful novelist but also became entangled in drug addiction, alcoholism, bulimia, and unhappy love affairs. Her friends were "brilliant hilarious progressive" people who would not comprehend someone in their circle turning to a faith like Christianity.

For someone like Ziya Meral, the cost of becoming a Christian would be even higher than facing the derision of skeptical friends and family, though he would encounter that adamant opposition. As a young man with a Muslim background living in Turkey, becoming a Christian would mean isolation, fear, economic deprivation, shame, loneliness, and the unlikelihood of marriage. Why would he put himself through this?

"Big Jim" Vaus made his living in the 1940s doing illegal wiretapping for Hollywood stars and later for organized crime boss Mickey Cohen. Expanding his work beyond bugging phones in high-profile divorce cases and other such work for politicians and businessmen, Vaus helped create a system to withhold horserace results from going out over the wire service for about ninety seconds so that bets could be illegally placed. This lucrative criminal activity would certainly not be compatible with Christianity. For Vaus, becoming a Christian not only would mean a change of occupation but also would require repentance, restitution, and the possibility of retaliation by the mobsters he was leaving behind. Why would a career criminal even consider such a move?

Jesus Shows Up and Changes Everything

Each of those individuals became a Christian; none sought God. Instead, they and others like them describe a process of God pursuing them, and His presence was not always welcome. As another reluctant convert, C. S. Lewis, put it, "Amiable agnostics will talk cheerfully about 'man's search for God.' To me, as I then was, they might as well have talked about the mouse's search for the cat."[3]

When Anne Lamott sensed the presence of Jesus in her room, she was in distinctly unreligious circumstances. Leading up to that night, she had hit a crisis with her alcohol and drug use. She believed she would die soon, but "out of nowhere" it crossed her mind to speak to a priest at a nearby Episcopal church whom some family friends had told her about. She did believe in God but said, "Mine was a patchwork of God, sewn together from bits of rag and ribbon, Eastern and Western, pagan and Hebrew, everything but the kitchen sink and Jesus."[4] Her discussions with the priest helped push her a little further toward belief, and not long afterward she began attending St. Andrew Presbyterian Church in Marin City, California, because she liked the music she heard coming out of it as she walked by on Sunday mornings. She stayed only for the music and left before the sermon was preached.

Anne became pregnant around this time, had an abortion, and that's when Jesus showed up. Weak from bleeding and "shaky and sad and too wild to have another drink or take a sleeping pill," she lay in bed and became aware of the presence of someone in the room with her. "The feeling was so strong that I actually turned on the light for a moment to make sure no one was there—of course there wasn't. But after a while, in the dark again, I knew beyond any doubt that it was Jesus. I felt him as surely as I feel my dog lying nearby as I write this." Even now, she did not welcome Him. She was "appalled," worried about what her friends would think if she became a Christian. Her conversion seemed "an utterly impossible thing that simply could not be allowed to happen. I turned to the wall and said out loud, 'I would rather die.'"[5] She felt Jesus with her there all night, watching her in patience and love, but she did not invite Him into her life until a week later, alone in her houseboat.

For Sara Miles, it was also an encounter with Jesus—unexpected, unsought—that transformed her. One day out of curiosity she walked into St. Gregory's Episcopal Church in San Francisco. "I had no earthly reason to be there. I'd never heard a gospel reading, never said the Lord's Prayer. I was certainly not interested in becoming a Christian—or, as I thought of it rather less politely, a religious nut." She looked around, admired the beauty of the church's interior, and took a seat, hoping no one would notice her. She sang with everyone else, feeling a little ridiculous, and then a woman announced, "Jesus invites everyone to His table."

Miles went forward and stood at the table. After more singing, someone put a "piece of fresh, crumbly bread in my hands, saying, 'the body of Christ,' and handed me the goblet of sweet wine, saying, 'the blood of Christ,' and then something outrageous and terrifying happened. Jesus happened to me."

That was Miles' moment of conversion, but it so bewildered her that she immediately sought alternate explanations. The word "Jesus" lodged in her mind, and she said it over and over, not knowing why. "But it was realer than any thought of mine, or even any subjective emotion: It was as real as the actual taste of the bread and the wine. And the word was indisputably in my body now, as if I'd swallowed a radioactive pellet that would outlive my own flesh."[6]

What About All Those Unanswered Questions?

It's one thing to have a dramatic encounter with Jesus in a heightened spiritual moment, but what happens to these reluctant Christian converts once the moment fades and they have time to rethink it? What happens the next day? Or a week later? Or a year after the event? They're still the same skeptical, intelligent people who had rejected Christianity for years, so wouldn't a strong impulse rise to explain away what had happened to them?

Or what happens when the costs start to kick in? How do these resistant believers face the scorn of that first friend to whom they declare, "I have become a Christian," contradicting everything they have stood for up to that point? What happens to these God-pursued converts when their decision to be a follower of Jesus threatens their livelihoods or their very lives? In purely human terms, wouldn't it make sense for them to reconsider or redefine their experience or, in the interests of self-preservation, let the incident fade away?

The whole process by which resistant believers find God—or He finds them—is nothing like what I would expect. These people have strong objections to Christianity. They have a lifetime of experience and training that has helped them compile a long list of reasons they should stay away from this religion and the followers who practice it. What I would expect, then, is that before they came to Christ, they would seek some opportunity to present these objections and doubts and get solid answers to them. Why, they might ask, is Christianity better than any other way of communing with a higher power? Why should they turn to Christ when most of their friends do fine without Him? The list of objections would vary for each person, but everyone would have plenty of questions. Only after each objection on the list had been checked off as adequately answered could they safely give their lives to Jesus Christ.

It rarely happens that way.

Jesus catches people mid-stream. Sometimes He shows up when they least expect and least want Him. Sometimes He finds them when they're children, sometimes when they're on their deathbed. Some of their objections to Him may have been answered, but many others remain, and many have not even occurred to them yet. But there He is, His presence loving and patient and inviting. And they either accept His invitation or they don't.

Believers aren't people who have answered every question about Jesus. They are people who have met Him.

A Grip So Powerful They Can't Escape It

One thing I love about these stories is that once these skeptical believers finally confront the God who has lodged himself inconveniently on their paths, the experience is so transforming that they can't turn away from Him even when every other circumstance cries out for them to do so.

Turkish Muslim Ziya Meral was only seventeen years old when against all expectations he encountered Christ on a visit to an Anglican church he went to after reading a derogatory article about the church in a newspaper. How could he possibly tell his family about his conversion? He says, "I remember how fearful I was and how isolated and alone I felt as I lay in the fetal position in a sleeping bag on a friend's floor."

Not a heartwarming introduction to the Christian life. And his spiritual journey has never gotten easier. Many years later Meral writes, "I am still broke, sober, and single after all these years, and I still struggle with shame, loneliness, and fear." At times the cost of being a Christian has been almost unbearable. "Twice," Meral says, "I came close to giving up my faith. On one of those occasions, I genuinely doubted whether or not Jesus was worth all the pain, and on the other I struggled with my commitment to work in the Middle East and the continuous price I pay, when I could have easily settled into a comfortable Christian life in a Western country."

What keeps him going? Jesus grips him so powerfully that Meral defines his own suffering as a way to identify with Christ: "But our highest good is not a problem-free life; it is to be like the Son." He quotes the scripture written by Paul—another believer who suffered greatly—that says,

> We always carry around in our body the death of Jesus, so that the life of Jesus may also be revealed in our body. For we who are alive are always being given over to death for Jesus' sake, so that his life may be revealed in our mortal body. So then, death is at work in us, but life is at work in you (*2 Corinthians 4:10-12*).

Meral has every earthly reason not to be a Christian. To most people around him who do not share his belief, his decision to be a Christian undoubtedly makes no sense at all. But what Meral cannot escape—even in the midst of pain, isolation, and persecution—is the life-giving presence of the Holy Spirit. He writes,

> We do know where God is in the midst of persecution. He is there, right with us, in us. He is present through our lives, words, pain, and deaths. . . . He is not distant from our pain; he is in prison with us, he is naked, he is beaten, he is raped, and he is killed! We know that he is not quiet, but is speaking powerfully through the lives, suffering, and death of his children.[7]

Even Under Enormous Stress, Their Faith Holds

What inspires me about radically transformed believers like Meral, Miles, and Lamott is how they maintain their faith in the isolated, private moments that never make it into a memoir or article—moments when fellow Christians hurt them or disappoint them, times when they're outraged by the actions of fellow believers on the opposite end of the political spectrum, times of weariness, when doubt creeps in and when, in the midst of the annoying and exhausting difficulties of life, Jesus seems simply too remote even to be real.

Most Christians go through periods like that, but I'm inclined to think that for the reluctant convert who didn't want to be a Christian in the first place and who is daily already paying a price for it, these times of discouragement would be particularly dangerous. That's when they would be tempted to think, *My friends were right! I never should have converted to this faith. These Christians are just as bad as I was warned they would be. I've made a fool of myself. I need to get out of this!*

Opportunities for exiting the faith exist at every turn. No believer *has* to remain a Christian, least of all those with so many incentives not to believe. These reluctant believers, pursued by God, stay in, because deep within them is the love and the presence of a Savior more powerful and more sustaining than the doubts that afflict them.

"Big Jim" Vaus, considered as organized crime's best wire-tapper, was assigned to go to St. Louis in November 1949 to work on a major project for his mob bosses. He never made it. Instead, he took a detour to a Billy Graham crusade in Los Angeles. As Vaus's son Will describes it,

> That night Graham preached on the passage in the gospels in which Jesus queried, "What shall it profit a man if he shall gain the whole world but lose his own soul?" My father felt as if God were speaking directly to him. He committed his life to Jesus Christ that night and immediately set about repaying everyone he had ever cheated or from whom he had stolen.[8]

For a career criminal, especially one employed by gangsters with no reluctance to kill people who cross them, becoming a Christian is extremely inconvenient and dangerous. Restitution is not easy. How many times throughout that long process must Vaus have been tempted to second-guess his commitment to Christ? What about when he told ruthless mob boss Mickey Cohen he could no longer work for him? What about when he later had to testify against Cohen in court? What about when he changed his own false testimony that he had given to a grand jury, which had led to an innocent police officer being jailed? Was the possibility of being prosecuted for perjury—assuming one of his enemies didn't kill him first—worth it in order to be a follower of Jesus Christ?

At any step of the way, Vaus could have retreated to his old lifestyle. He could have played it safe. His commitment to pay back those from whom he had stolen cost him dearly. His son writes, "My parents sold almost all of their worldly assets: car, house and furniture. When Dad had finished going through his restitution list of thirty some odd people, he and Mom had nothing left but the clothes on their backs, but at least Dad was able to repay everyone who asked for it."[9]

Vaus could have made it easier on himself. He at least could have kept silent about his faith and decided not to repay those he had stolen from. But he was pursued by a God who was bigger than the threat of money problems or prison or retaliation. As he told one reporter, "Jim Vaus is dead. . . . The man you were looking for, the one who used to do wiretapping and sell the recordings to the highest bidder, that man is dead. I'm a new man. It's like the Bible says: 'If any man be in Christ, he is a new creature.'"[10]

God Is Out to Get Us

If God pursues and finds Vaus and the other reluctant converts mentioned in this chapter—people with cultural, social, political, moral, and criminal reasons to avoid Him—then who can be said to be beyond His grasp? For whom is it safe to conclude, *this* person is too far from God to ever reach Him? This one is too hostile toward Him—too vulgar, too sarcastic and dismissive, too evil.

The question of who is too far gone for God to reach is a question people have been asking for centuries. They even asked Jesus essentially the same thing. It was couched as a nasty comment. Luke 15:1 says that the "tax collectors and 'sinners' were all gathering around to hear" Jesus. Instead of being happy that the truth of Jesus' message was so powerful that it could attract even these unlikely followers, "the Pharisees and the teachers of the law muttered, 'This man welcomes sinners and eats with them'" (Luke 15:2). How scandalous! The religious elite didn't want God pursuing *those* people. If He lets *them* in, then who could possibly be excluded?

Jesus answered their muttering with the stories of the lost sheep, the lost coin, and the lost son, better known as the story of the prodigal son. All three stories are about lost things that are doggedly pursued by a determined person who values them. In the first one a shepherd has a hundred sheep and loses one of them. He leaves the ninety-nine to pursue the lost one, and then he calls his friends and neighbors together to rejoice once he finds it. In the next story a woman has ten silver coins and loses one. She searches until she finds it; then she celebrates with friends and neighbors.

You might think that for God, ninety-nine out of a hundred sheep would be enough. Nine out of ten coins should be plenty. What's one sheep or one coin more or less when you have so many? Plenty of people seek God voluntarily and then devote their whole lives to Him. So why would He bother putting forth so much effort to find people like Anne Lamott, Ziya Meral, Jim Vaus? Or me? Or you? Yet I feel that pursuing Spirit of God moving deep within me. I'm grateful because I know I'm the lost coin He'll turn the house upside down to find. I'm the lost sheep He'll search the countryside to hunt down. I'm grateful that finding God does not depend on my effort alone. Even if I'm hostile, deluded, full of sin, indifferent, He still wants me. Even when I'm running away or merely standing still, He is still running toward me, arms outstretched.

A Father running with arms outstretched is at the heart of Jesus' most famous parable—perhaps the most famous parable ever told. The story is usually labeled that of the prodigal son, but it could also be called the story of the rebellious son, the lost sons, or even better, the forgiving father or the pursuing father. The younger of two sons runs away from his father and squanders his share of the estate in wild living, burning his bridges to his family in the process. The father has no further obligation to him. The son has made his choice, and now in all fairness he should have to live with the consequences.

The rebellious son ends up hungry, poverty-stricken, regretful. He comes to his senses. Out of options, he decides to slink back to his father and offer to work for him as a hired man. That's the best he can realistically hope for, and even that outcome is more than the father is morally or legally obligated to give.

Slinking Back to Dad

I know the humiliation of having to creep back to my father after having messed up in a big way. I got my driver's license when I was sixteen. I had a job after school, so my dad gave me his old car and got another one for himself. It was a generous thing for him to do, and it also helped him avoid another problem he didn't want to deal with—he didn't want me borrowing his car. Dad was finicky about his cars. They were spotless, well-maintained, beautifully cared for. He didn't want some teenager, or anybody else, getting in there and messing them up. The car he gave me still belonged to him, and he expected me to be careful with it. Reverence for cars had long been a part of a household in which both my dad and sister worked for General Motors and where my dad had restored old cars.

That made my careless and stupid wreck all the more embarrassing. It happened in our neighborhood, and my car was the only one involved, so I had no one but myself to blame. I was a terrible driver. To get out of the neighborhood, I had to make a narrow turn—or at least it seemed narrow to me—at a street where a guardrail jutted out at a right angle. If I turned too wide, my car would go into the wrong lane of the street I was turning onto and hit any oncoming cars. If I turned too sharply, I would hit the corner of the guardrail.

I turned too sharply. The guardrail sliced into the passenger door like the iceberg ripping into the *Titanic*. At that point I should have stopped. I could have backed away from the guardrail and limited the damage. Instead, out of panic, or some irrational hope of pulling away from the rail by moving forward, I kept going, and I heard the scraping of metal all the way to the end of the car.

I pulled to the side of the road and felt the cold layer of sweat wash over me. I got out to inspect the damage. Maybe it wasn't as bad as I feared. Maybe it was just a scratch that I could buff out without even telling Dad.

It was bad. The door and fender were caved in beyond all buffing. I could not wish this away. I could not deny this or blame somebody else for it or defend it. I had to take the car home and show Dad what a stupid thing I had done. What would it cost me? How could I bring myself to tell him to come out to the driveway to look? I stood for a long time in silence and stared at my mangled car.

He Should Turn His Back on You, But Instead . . .

This brings me back to the story of the prodigal son. You know how the story ends, but don't let the familiarity of it blind you from its power. Perhaps you're the rebellious son. You don't want to creep back to your father. This was not your plan. You're not sure you can make yourself do it. Your attitudes toward your father change from moment to moment. Sometimes you *fear* him because of what you've done, but at other times you *resent* him because you're in this humiliating position toward him. Shouldn't he have done more to prevent you from getting into such a mess? He didn't *have* to give you your inheritance. Isn't this his fault as much as yours?

You *dread* him one moment, but in the next you realize he's your only hope. Sometimes you want to run to him and get it over with, then think maybe a slow death would be better.

Finally you edge toward him, but at any moment you may change your mind and run in the other direction. Then something completely unexpected happens. Against cultural tradition, protocol, fairness, and good sense, your father does not wait for you to reach him. He should stay home and let you beg. Forgiving you at that point would be magnanimous enough. Instead, he loves you so much that the moment he sees you, the moment he knows you're headed in his direction, he *runs to meet you*. You won't arrive home alone. He'll usher you in. As Luke 15:20 puts it, "While he was still a long way off, his father saw him and was filled with compassion for him; he ran to his son, threw his arms around him and kissed him."

This is not the painful homecoming you expected. The father throws a celebration for you. You get the best robe, a ring for your finger, and sandals for your feet. You'll eat the fattened calf at your party. The extravagance is downright embarrassing. You don't deserve all this.

Timothy Keller, who has written an insightful book on this parable, points out that the word "prodigal" does not mean *wayward*, but "'recklessly spendthrift.' It means spending until you have nothing left. This term is therefore as appropriate for describing the father in the story as his younger son. The father's welcome to the repentant son was literally reckless, because he refused to 'reckon' or count his sin against him or demand repayment."[11]

When I think back to how my father reacted when I crept back home to show him his car I had so stupidly wrecked, he reacted with more restraint and patience than I deserved, which was a big relief to me. But I had to live with the consequences of my actions. I drove around in a smashed-in car for the next few years.

The father's action in the prodigal son story would be like my father looking at my wrecked car and saying, "Look what you've done! Now that this car is damaged, let me take you out to the dealership right now and buy you a brand new sports car." No one—least of all me—would expect that kind of magnanimous reaction to a son smashing up a car that had been given to him. Many would even call it bad, reckless parenting to buy the son a new car in such a case. And what would my sister say if she pulled into our driveway in her carefully preserved junker and saw that Dad had bought me a new Corvette after I had plowed my old car into a guard rail?

God's love, His forgiveness, His pursuit, goes far beyond common sense, far beyond what we would do or what we would expect any reasonable God to do. I was far from God, I was dreading Him, but He ran after me, hugged me, lavished me with gifts, and prepared a party.

Sara Miles heard the same message on the day she was told, "Jesus invites everyone to His table." She ate and drank and was home. The same Jesus hunkered down in Anne Lamott's room as she lay shaky from bleeding in the aftermath of an abortion and drinking and drugs. He chased her down, and she let Him in. The same God ran to Jim Vaus as the wire-tapper took what he thought was a quick detour to a Billy Graham crusade on his way to commit another crime.

It's so easy to identify with the rebellious younger brother in Jesus' parable that I usually don't give much thought to the older brother. But Keller shows that the older brother, the "good" one, also rebels and has just as much need for the father's pursuing, patient love as the young one.

The older brother feels cheated and demeans his father by refusing to go in to the feast. The pursuing father comes out to him to urge him to come in, but the son refuses to speak respectfully to him. As Keller explains, "He refuses to address him in the elaborately respectful manner that inferiors owed superiors in that culture, particularly in public. He does not say 'esteemed father' but simply 'Look!'—which is equivalent to 'Look, you!'"[12]

What is the significance of this older son's rebellion? No one, not even the "good" people who follow all the rules, can earn salvation through good deeds. Only God's initiating love can save them.

Keller writes of this man, "Pride in his good deeds, rather than remorse over his bad deeds, was keeping the older son out of the feast of salvation. The elder brother's problem is his self-righteousness, the way he uses his moral record to put God and others in his debt to control them to do what he wants."[13]

Will he drop his rebellion and respond to the father's love? The story doesn't say. The Pharisees and other "older brother" types in Jesus' audience, both then and now, would have to decide how their own stories would end.

"Your Beauty and Love Chase After Me."

Even as a long-time Christian, I still feel God's loving pursuit. In one sense, my faith, and the continued existence of the entire Christian Church, for that matter, hangs by a frail thread. I could walk away whenever I want. Belief in Christ and my ties to the Church do not bind me legally and contractually in the same way, for instance, that I am legally bound to my wife and children or my job, or even my mortgage. I recently started serving on our church board, and one of the first duties was to approve the budget for the following year. As I reviewed the rows of numbers detailing the budget lines for children's ministries and building funds and salaries, the thought occurred to me, *What if all these people giving this money—or even half of them—suddenly walked away?* No one is forcing them to stay in the church or to keep giving even if they do stay. Only a couple of people in the church even *know* how much individuals give.

Some people do drop out, but the vast majority stay. They keep coming to church, keep giving, keep believing in Christ, keep trying to follow Him better. People get offended, they hurt each other's feelings, they do things they shouldn't and have to keep asking for forgiveness, but still they keep believing, keep coming back. Sometimes my own skepticism flares up, I get angry with the church, I get bored or bogged down with difficulties or feel unappreciated or misunderstood. Quitting is a temptation, but someone deeper than all those problems—the pursuing, loving, embracing Holy Spirit— keeps me and my fellow believers connected to Him and the church with a deep bond. No matter how discouraged I get, God's deeper sustaining love and purpose hold on to me. As Eugene Peterson paraphrases a verse from Psalm 23,

> Your beauty and love chase after me
> every day of my life.
> I'm back in the house of Yahweh
> for the rest of my life (Psalm 23:6, TM).

I wish I could keep the image of God the Pursuer more consistently in my thoughts. I spend much of my Christian life striving to prove myself to Him by working to make up for past misdeeds. There are so many things I don't understand but want to. There are so many ways I fail but wish I didn't. Can I follow Jesus with integrity? Do my spiritual weaknesses disqualify me? It's a comfort to know I'm not in some competition in which only the strongest and most competent survive. God still wants me—not just *accepts* me but is actively searching me out—even if I'm that hundredth sheep lost out there in the bushes while everybody else seems to have known enough to stay in the fold. And when He finds me, His attitude is not to berate me or make me pay, but instead He calls everyone together and celebrates.

When it comes to God pursuing a reluctant convert, one person has a story no one else can match. We'll consider his miraculous encounter with God—and what it means for the rest of us—in the next chapter.

Go to www.beaconhillbooks.com/go/godinpursuit for a free downloadable Study Guide that includes questions for deeper personal reflection as well as activities for use in a small-group setting.

TWO

Awakened
Light and Foreshadow

It's easy to be envious of the apostle Paul's conversion story. The clarity and suddenness of it are remarkable. A flash of light and a voice from heaven, and his life changed forever. Unlike many others who inch their way toward conversion, sometimes for years, Paul didn't have to struggle with long periods of spiritual seeking, agonizing prayer, spasms of doubt, debates with friends.

Paul, or Saul, as he was called at this point in his story, had walked down the road toward Damascus with a definite purpose in mind. He had intended to round up Christians there and drag them back to Jerusalem as prisoners. His plans changed on that road when

> suddenly a light from heaven flashed around him. He fell to the ground and heard a voice say to him, "Saul, Saul, why do you persecute me?"
>
> "Who are you, Lord?" Saul asked.
>
> "I am Jesus, whom you are persecuting," he replied. "Now get up and go into the city, and you will be told what you must do" (*Acts 9:3-6*).

Blinded for three days as a result of this event, Paul hobbled to Damascus with his friends. He had nothing to eat or drink as he wait-

ed for instructions. Those orders came from a disciple named Annanias, who had received a vision in which the Lord told him, "This
man is my chosen instrument to carry my name before the Gentiles
and their kings and before the people of Israel. I will show him how
much he must suffer for my name" (Acts 9:15-16). Once Annanias
delivered the message, something like scales fell from Paul's eyes, he
could see again, and he got up and was baptized. After several days
with the disciples in Damascus, "At once he began to preach in the
synagogues that Jesus is the Son of God" (Acts 9:20).

Paul went from fervent persecutor of Christians to passionate
believer in Christ in a matter of minutes, and he began a ministry
that would determine the shape of much of the New Testament and
alter the course of world history only days later. A beautiful, crisp
story, nothing like the more complex and meandering conversion
experiences so many of us have. It's also nothing like the relatively
uneventful conversions that are far more common.

But the startling power of Paul's transformation should not ob-
scure the fact that like Anne Lamott, Jim Vaus, and others discussed
in the previous chapter, Paul did not want to become a Christian.
Like those others, he had a long list of reasons why becoming a follower of Christ would be a very bad idea. For one thing, how would
he explain such a radical shift to his friends? It's not just that he
didn't *believe* in Christianity—it's that he wanted to *wipe it out*.
And now he was going to drop those plans and preach the gospel?

He also faced the problem of how to explain his shift to his
former enemies, the Christians themselves. Wouldn't they be suspi-
cious—one minute he wanted to kill them, and the next he wanted to *join* them? Annanias expressed this doubt about Paul to the
Lord: "I have heard many reports about this man and all the harm
he has done to your saints in Jerusalem. And he has come here with
authority from the chief priests to arrest all who call on your name"
(Acts 9:13-14). Even if Paul could win the trust of other Christians,

how would he handle his own internal upheaval, becoming an advocate of everything he once despised?

Then there's that word from the Lord that Annanias delivered. Did Jesus say, "I want to let Paul know how he's going to change history"? or "I want to give him a sense of how many people throughout the world are going to become my disciples because of his letters"? No, the Lord's message was "I will show him how much he must suffer for my name." Not much of a recruiting pitch. And suffer Paul did—beatings, arrests, imprisonment, riots, arguments, persecutions of every kind, plots against his life, shipwreck, death. He knew the suffering was coming. He followed anyway.

Jerome Murphy-O'Connor writes, "The brutality of the 180-degree turn-around is evoked by Paul when he says, 'I was apprehended by Christ Jesus' (Phil. 3:12). With irresistible power Jesus arrested him and set him on a completely different path."[1]

The Essence of Conversion

Richard V. Peace says the "sudden" conversion of this reluctant follower of Christ contains within it "crucial insight into the nature of conversion itself." Paul's conversion story is told three times in Acts, and the third time Paul adds more details about the mission to the Gentiles that Jesus is assigning him to fulfill. Paul says Jesus told him, "I am sending you to them to open their eyes and turn them from darkness to light, and from the power of Satan to God, so that they may receive forgiveness of sins and a place among those who are sanctified by faith in me" (Acts 26:17-18).

Peace finds in that statement not only the essence of Paul's own conversion but also the basic elements of Christian conversion itself. First, for any convert there is *seeing*. Paul's eyes were opened to who Jesus is, and he was being sent to open the eyes of the Gentiles. Next there is *turning*. Paul turned from darkness to light, from being a persecutor of Christians to being an advocate of the faith, and he would urge others to make that same turn. Finally, there is *transformation* in the form of forgiveness of sins and a new life of discipleship in Jesus.[2]

Paul didn't simply turn away from his old life and toward the new. He also acted on that commitment, being baptized, spending time learning from fellow Christians, and then beginning his preaching.

Those three elements—seeing, turning, and transformation—are the basics of conversion whether sudden or slow. The *suddenness* of Paul's conversion, Peace says, comes in the first part, the *seeing* or insight, which happened in an instant. He writes, "Perhaps this is what ought to distinguish sudden conversion from other forms of conversion, not the rapid turning as much as the suddenness of insight. The turning follows almost by reflex when the insight is there: insight into truth, God, oneself, Jesus, the way the world works."[3]

The instantaneousness of the conversions discussed so far is what makes the stories so dramatic. But are these conversions really as sudden as they look, or had key incidents in the lives of Paul and others prepared the moment of Christ's arrival in ways the future converts were not aware of?

Foreshadowing: How God Plants Clues on the Path to Faith

One unlikely Christian who helped me better understand the conversions of Paul and other reluctant converts is Lauren Winner, author of *Girl Meets God*. Winner converted from Judaism, and at first it may look as if her more gradual movement toward Christ has little in common with Paul's experience. She writes, "Evangelical friends of mine are always trying to trim the corners and smooth the rough edges of what they call My Witness in order to shove it into a tidy, born-again conversion narrative. They want an exact date, even an hour, and I never know what to tell them." She had no "epiphanic on-the-road-to-Damascus experience."[4]

Winner's years-long movement toward Christ includes elements harder to fit into a neat conversion narrative than Paul's blinding light and voice of Jesus. God put clues in her path all along the way, signs that pointed her toward Him, a process she calls foreshadowing. She explains, "God is a novelist. He uses all sorts of literary devices: alliteration, assonance, rhyme, synecdoche, onomatopoeia. But of all these, His favorite is foreshadowing."[5]

In Winner's life, the foreshadowing—clues as to where the story is headed—took many forms over the years. Books she read, a gold cross she had asked her mother to buy her at age eleven, a chance conversation with a fundamentalist Christian during her junior year of high school, and many other clues foreshadowed her eventual turn to Christ.

One experience that brought her closer to belief in Jesus, for instance, was a powerful dream in which she and her friends were kidnapped by a band of mermaids. After a year they were rescued by a group of men, including a "beautiful, thirtyish, dark Daniel-Day-Lewis-like man." She went home to her fiancé and prepared for her fast-approaching wedding, but she also slipped off occasionally to talk to her rescuer about the kidnapping. Winner was used to vivid dreams, but as soon as she awoke, she knew this one was different. She knew "the dream had come from God and it was about the reality of Jesus. The truth of Him. That He was a person whose pronouns you had to capitalize. That He was God. I knew that with more certainty than I have ever known anything else."[6]

Although most people may not experience anything as bizarre as that dream, most of us who are Christians will understand exactly what Winner means by spiritual foreshadowing. As we look back on the influences that led us to Christ, they are often small things that didn't seem significant at the time—an overheard song from a car across the street, a phrase in a sermon that only we seemed to notice, a portion of Scripture we can't get out of our heads. Winner says, "Sometimes, as in a great novel, you cannot see until you get to the end that God was leaving clues for you all along. Sometimes you wonder, *How did I miss it? Surely any idiot should have been able to see from the second chapter that it was Miss Scarlet in the conservatory with the rope.*"[7]

The Tiniest Clue May Foreshadow Faith

I was six years old. My family did not attend church. One weekend my Uncle Mervin, who visited us frequently from out of town, invited me to go to church with him at a new church building that had been constructed near our house. I liked going to church with him and often did so when we were visiting him, but I was afraid of this new place. Looking back, I know that my particular fear was not rational, but I vividly remember how strong it was at the time.

My fear was that my uncle would drop me off for children's Sunday School in this vast new place while he went to his own class. Since I didn't know anybody there and had never been there, I knew I would wander around the corridors lost for the whole morning. Even worse, I feared that I would somehow get in trouble for not being in the right place and would be punished. I didn't tell my uncle or anyone else what I was afraid of, but it almost kept me from going with him.

Still, I went. Even though this happened forty years ago, I clearly remember walking into the church foyer that day, frightened of what might happen next and wishing I could turn back. I also can clearly picture the woman who walked up to us, clipboard in hand, and welcomed us to the church. She talked to my uncle for a few minutes, wrote down some information, and then leaned over and spoke to me. To my huge relief, she then led me to my classroom and introduced me to the teacher and to the other kids. My fear dissolved. I loved the teacher and the class. My uncle picked me up at the end of class and took me to the worship service. I wanted to keep going to that church, and I did. Two years later, I became a

Christian there during Vacation Bible School. I was baptized there, became a member, and kept attending until I went to college.

A lady with a clipboard, making a child feel comfortable in church—it was routine for her. She probably forgot about it immediately, but forty years later it is still vivid in my mind. When I look back on it, I see her kind invitation into a church classroom as a foreshadowing of the invitation to follow Christ that would happen two years later. Like the church itself, she kindly and gently led me toward Christ. Her welcoming gesture was the first act of a church that said, *Come on in. You're welcome here. Come meet Jesus.*

I now wonder—what if she hadn't been there that day? What if she had been too busy to bother with some little kid? What if I had walked away from that church wanting nothing more to do with it? How long might it have been before I ever tried another?

I got to know that lady, whose name is Doris, over the years that I grew up in that church, but I never told her the part she played in my conversion. I doubt she ever suspected she had anything to do with it. Did my uncle know the significance of his action when he invited me that day? Did the teacher sense the impact she was having on a boy when she made me feel welcome and told the Bible stories that burned brightly in my imagination? How often may any of us be part of the foreshadowing—one of God's planted clues—on someone's path to Jesus Christ? Even our smallest acts, words, and attitudes may matter more than we may ever realize.

Even "Sudden" Conversions May Be Years in the Making

In one sense Paul's story doesn't appear to contain any foreshadowing. His was the quintessential "sudden" conversion, a transformation from murderous hostility to radical embrace of Christ in one shining moment. But viewed from a different perspective, nearly everything that happened to Paul leading up to his conversion helped make him ready for it and also prepared him for the work he would do as an apostle and as the author of a large portion of the New Testament.

If God wanted to call someone to reach the Gentiles with the gospel, choosing a Christian-hating Pharisee like Paul might seem an odd choice, but Paul's education and background in Roman, Greek, and Jewish cultures prepared him perfectly. Look how Udo Schnelle explains the way this blending of backgrounds helped shape Paul's Christian ministry:

> Paul was a citizen of the Roman Empire who had grown up in a significant cultural metropolis of the realm, had disciplined himself in an intensive Pharisaic education (possibly in Jerusalem), and had worked for about three decades in a province of the empire where Hellenistic culture prevailed. . . . Both his educational experience and his ability to enter into the intellectual horizon of his various audiences show the breadth of the apostle's formation. This ability gave Paul access to a broad spectrum of social groups and classes and predestined him to cross social and geographical boundaries in order to win people to the gospel.[8]

As a writer, Paul benefited from his education in Greek rhetoric. Jerome Murphy-O'Connor explains,

> The quality of Paul's secular education is manifest not only in his command of Greek, but in the way in which he organized the content of his letters. . . . His mastery of the figures of style, and the rhetorical structure of his letters, can only have been the fruit of serious study and long practice. His grasp of the principles of persuasive presentation was so sure that he could even parody them.[9]

Beyond the style of his writing, Paul's background as a devout Pharisee, including his intimate knowledge of the Hebrew Scriptures, formed a solid basis for his theology. Schnelle shows in great detail a wide range of concepts that Paul draws on from his Jewish background, such as his concepts of election, righteousness, sin, justification, covenant, the Judgment, resurrection, and others.[10] Paul extended these ideas into a Christian understanding, but his years of education and practice as a Pharisee turned out to be preparation for his work as a Christian writer, preacher, and thinker.

Paul's zeal as a Jew also foreshadowed his intense commitment as a Christian. In his letter to the Galatians he writes, "You have heard of my previous way of life in Judaism, how intensely I persecuted the church of God and tried to destroy it. I was advancing in Judaism beyond many Jews of my own age and was extremely zealous for the traditions of my fathers" (Galatians 1:13-14). That unswerving devotion to his cause was an absolute necessity when he converted to Christianity and faced the constant threat of imprisonment and death. Even Paul's persecution of Christians foreshadowed his conversion to the faith, because his obsession to destroy it meant that he had to learn many of its beliefs.

Some people feel inclined toward God from an early age, but even for the more reluctant or hostile converts like those discussed in the previous chapter, foreshadowing is evident in every story. Listen to how Anne Lamott, for instance, describes God's foreshadowing in her own life:

> My coming to faith did not start with a leap but rather a series of staggers from what seemed like one safe place to another. Like lily pads, round and green, these places summoned and then held me up while I grew. Each prepared me for the next leaf on which I would land, and in this way I moved across the swamp of doubt and fear.[11]

Although LaMott was raised as an atheist, other influences—lily pads, clues, foreshadowing—were scattered across her path. As a girl she had friends who took her to a Catholic church, which she loved. In college she read Thomas Merton, Simone Weil, William Blake, Rumi. She read Kierkegaard's *Fear and Trembling* and took a leap of faith into believing in God, but not yet Christianity.

As mentioned earlier, she later met an Episcopal minister who helped her a little farther down the road to belief, and she found a church whose music she liked even though she wouldn't stay for the sermons. Individually, many of these clues did not reveal their meaning at the time; she could not have imagined where her story was headed. She had no idea that God was seeking her.

Sara Miles's abrupt conversion when she wandered into a church and received her first Communion sounds completely un-foreshadowed, but, in fact, her path was strewn with clues. Examples abound, but I'll mention one briefly. Miles serves in a church that collects and gives away several tons of food each week to needy people. Her own conversion centered not on ideas about Christianity but on food—the bread and wine served at Communion. One of her early jobs was working as a cook in various restaurants, so preparing and serving food to people have been an important part of her background and helped to foreshadow her Christian ministry.

Thinking back to her work at one of the restaurants, she remembered how even then she realized how crucial food was to gathering people together and creating a sense of community. She writes, "As a wise bishop would tell me, years and years later, in words I couldn't possibly have grasped back then, 'There's a hunger beyond food that's expressed in food, and that's why feeding is always a kind of miracle.'"[12]

Foreshadowing doesn't end at conversion. Throughout our Christian lives, God plants clues that may seem insignificant to us at the time but later turn out to be key pieces of our puzzle. Right now the frustrating job we're forced to work may seem like an irritating detour from the path we thought we were following, but it may fit God's plan for us in ways that will make sense only years from now. The painful illness that now feels like nothing more than infuriating distraction may need to be reinterpreted someday when it yields its spiritual fruit. God is everywhere at work, carefully and often silently preparing us for those crucial, *seemingly* sudden moments of insight when it will be time for us to respond.

Loaded Time

As I've read and heard dozens of stories of people's conversions to Christianity, one fascinating mystery, especially in the lives of reluctant converts, is why the conversions happen when they do. Why not a week before or a week later—or years before or years later?

In some cases there do appear to be identifiable reasons why the time is particularly appropriate. When Jim Vaus took a break from his criminal activity for the mob in order to attend a Billy Graham crusade and turn his life over to Christ, what he did not know was that if he had instead gone to St. Louis as planned, he would have been killed by a rival gang that was out to get him.[13] Although he didn't know it, his encounter with Christ that night was literally his last chance to repent before he was executed.

With other people the timing is not so clear. Why did Anne Lamott give in to Jesus at the door of her houseboat a week after she sensed His presence in the corner of her room? Why not earlier that morning when she was in church? Why not a week before when she sensed His presence so powerfully?

One important word in the Bible describing time for which there is no adequate English equivalent is the Greek term *kairos*. The word has a number of shades of meaning, but one that I found most helpful in understanding God's timing in conversion is the idea of "loaded time." Rhetoric scholar Dale L. Sullivan says *kairos* is used this way in John 7:6, when Jesus says, "My time [*kairos*] is not yet come," and also in 2 Corinthians 6:2, which reads, "Now is the time [*kairos*] of God's favor, now is the day of salvation."

Sullivan explains that this sense of *kairos* "can be distributed along a continuum of time lengths, from a single point to a season to a time of fulfillment, but they all suggest that there is an opportune time for something to occur, that there are special times determined by God, shown by God, and filled with God."[14]

Loaded time—moments, separated from all the ordinary minutes and seconds of life, when time is particularly filled not only with God's presence but also with the opportunity to reach Him. We can say yes, we can say no, but somehow all the foreshadowing, the clues, the prowling pursuit of God's Spirit has led us to this moment, and we must decide.

Because we cannot predict the arrival of the loaded moments, they may have a random feel to them when they arrive. Novelist Frederick Buechner was in his late twenties and had received some early literary acclaim when he moved to New York City in the early 1950s. One Sunday in April 1953 he went to hear a famous pastor named George Buttrick speak. Buechner was not a Christian, and he went to the church out of curiosity and because it happened to be on the same block as his apartment. On this particular morning Buttrick discussed the coronation of Queen Elizabeth II, contrasting it to the crowning of Christ in the heart of the Christian.

As Buechner recalls, the pastor said that unlike the queen's coronation, the coronation of Jesus took place among confession and tears—

> and then, as God was and is my witness, *great laughter*, he said. Jesus is crowned among confession and tears and great laughter, and at the phrase *great laughter*, for reasons that I have never satisfactorily understood, the great wall of China crumbled and Atlantis rose up out of the sea, and on Madison Avenue, at 73rd Street, tears leapt from my eyes as though I had been struck across the face.[15]

This was the beginning of Buechner's conversion. He followed up with Buttrick, who mentored him and later urged him to attend Union Theological Seminary. Buechner became an ordained minister and wrote a wide range of novels and nonfiction books, now steeped in his Christian perspective.

Why did one small phrase in a sermon move Buechner so deeply? Not even he knows. For him, those moments in that sermon were loaded time, *kairos*, and they were filled with the presence of the Holy Spirit. If he had heard the sermon a month earlier or five years later, would it have had the same impact? Later, when Buechner went back and read a written transcript of Buttrick's sermon, he discovered that the phrase "great laughter" did not even appear there, "so I can only assume that he must have dreamed it up at the last minute and adlibbed it—and on just such foolish, tenuous, holy threads as that, I suppose, hang the destinies of us all."[16]

Maybe Buttrick ad-libbed the words "great laughter," and maybe he didn't. The Holy Spirit can speak beyond the actual words of a minister. You can probably think of such "loaded times" in your own life, when the truth breaks through in ways it never has before, even though you may have heard the same basic message dozens of times. Or times when a song or a sermon or a Sunday school lesson or a book leaves everyone else cold but ignites a fire inside you. Maybe that's God breaking through, inviting you in. Maybe that's your *kairos*.

Look! Look!

At times it seems as if God is deliberately pursuing us by the most difficult method possible, as if He wants to leave no doubt that *He* is reaching us and that no other explanation is plausible. Buechner was fortunate to live on the same block where one of the greatest preachers in America carried out his ministry, but the "loaded moment" for Charles Spurgeon arrived on a morning when he ended up in a tiny church with one of the worst preachers ever.

Spurgeon would eventually become one of the greatest preachers of the nineteenth century, speaking to large crowds twice a week in his six-thousand-seat church in London. Each week his sermons were also published and distributed "by the ton" to thousands of readers.[17] But the circumstances of his conversion were decidedly more modest. Eventually he boiled down his spiritual transformation to one simple idea: "In my conversion, the very point lay in making the discovery that I had nothing to do but to look to Christ, and I should be saved."[18] Sounds simple, but getting there was not so easy.

Many of the converts discussed so far were kept at a distance from the gospel by atheist backgrounds or other circumstances, but this was not the case for Spurgeon. He writes that as a child he had tried for years to learn the way of salvation. He had been raised by Christian parents; he had read the Bible; he had heard the gospel preached hundreds of times. Why hadn't it sunk in? At first, after his conversion, Spurgeon thought maybe the preachers he had listened to had not really preached the true gospel. Finally he came to the conclusion that the problem was not in the preaching but in his hearing:

On looking back, I am inclined to believe that I had heard the gospel fully preached many hundreds of times before, and that this was the difference—that I then heard it as though I heard it not; and when I did hear it, the message may not have been any more clear in itself than it had been at former times, but the power of the Holy Spirit was present to open my ear, and to guide the message of my heart.[19]

Like many who have been raised in the church, Spurgeon was dulled to the Christian message because of its familiarity. His Spirit-filled moment, his *kairos*, came on a day when circumstances forced him out of that routine.

Spurgeon was headed to church on January 6, 1850, when a snowstorm made travel conditions so bad that he had to turn down a side street and settle for the only church he could find, a Primitive Methodist Chapel with only twelve or fifteen people in it. Like Buechner, who had wandered into a church down the block, or Sara Miles, who had ducked into a church out of curiosity, or Anne Lamott, who had entered a church because she liked the music that drifted out of it, Charles Spurgeon landed in an unfamiliar chapel that he never could have predicted he would ever enter.

Nothing about the place impressed him. He had heard of the Primitive Methodists, but all he knew about them was "how they sang so loudly that they made people's heads ache." He didn't mind that so much as long as he could hear a good sermon. Unfortunately, the minister did not show up that morning, apparently because he, too, had gotten snowed in.

Finally, "a very thin-looking man, a shoemaker, or tailor, or something of that sort" went to the pulpit to preach. Spurgeon is blunt about what he thought: "This man was really stupid." The poor man, forced to substitute for the pastor at the last minute and not being a preacher, stuck closely to his text, which was, "Look unto me, and be ye saved, all the ends of the earth."[20]

The sermon itself started out rather tediously and repetitively, focusing on the word "look," with lines such as "Now lookin' don't take a deal of pains. It ain't liftin' your foot to your finger; it is just, 'Look.' Well, a man needn't go to college to learn to look. You may be the biggest fool, and yet you can look. Anyone can look; even a child can look." The man went on this way for about ten minutes until he ran out of steam, and then, to Spurgeon's discomfort, he turned his focus to Spurgeon himself.

"Young man, you look very miserable," he said.

Spurgeon agreed, but he thought, "I had not been accustomed to have remarks made from the pulpit on my personal appearance before." The preacher did not let up but told Spurgeon he would continue to be miserable unless he obeyed the text, but if he did obey, he would be saved. The preacher lifted up his hands and shouted, "Young man, look to Jesus Christ! Look! Look! You have nothin' to do but to look and live."

Not a profound sermon. Spurgeon no doubt had heard dozens of messages far better, delivered by more qualified ministers, in more hospitable surroundings. But this was Spurgeon's "loaded moment." The Holy Spirit was there, and salvation would come not by eloquent words or an inspiring setting but by the power of God in the room.

Spurgeon doesn't know what else the preacher said through the rest of his sermon. He paid no attention, because all his focus was on that word "Look."

Oh! I looked until I could almost have looked my eyes away. There and then the cloud was gone, the darkness had rolled away and that moment I saw the sun; I could have risen that instant, and sung with the most enthusiastic of them, of the precious blood of Christ, and the simple faith which looks alone to Him.[21]

Charles Spurgeon went on to preach far better sermons than the one that led to his own conversion, and he was to become far more famous than the fill-in preacher whose name was never recorded. But on that snowy day in 1850, when the weather was so nasty that even the preacher didn't show up, and when Spurgeon might just as easily have stayed in bed or gone back home when he couldn't reach his destination, God the pursuer came to strip away all the spiritual blindness and over-familiarity and change a man's life forever.

Implications for Christians of a God Who Pursues

Most of the converts to Christianity discussed so far are people who either started out hostile to it or who ended up encountering Christ in a spiritually loaded moment seemingly by accident. Although these strange conversions may seem like an odd place to begin a discussion on the turning points between doubt and belief, I believe these stories are some of the most powerful examples of the amazing ways God gets hold of people, and they offer a strong challenge to critics of Christianity. It's one thing for those critics to dispute lifelong believers who *want* Christianity to be true and who have a vested interest in marshalling every argument they can think of to prove that it is. But what about those who *don't* want it to be true but who can't help but believe it anyway? What about those who, by temperament, background, social relationships, and political leanings, would feel more comfortable with atheism but who can't get away from the truth of the Spirit of God they have experienced directly for themselves?

The stories of these converts also inspire me because if there is hope for these resistant or "accidental" converts to find God, then isn't there hope for everyone, especially those who are seeking Him with all their might? As a Christian, I can't give up on anyone I'm praying for to turn to Jesus Christ. There's no corner so remote that He can't reach, no suffering so deep that His Spirit cannot penetrate it, no indifference so settled that He cannot shake it.

I also love the fact that I may be part of someone else's "loaded moment" of encountering Christ. God uses the most unlikely people in some of the strangest ways to accomplish His purposes, and I may be one of those. The "real" preacher was snowed in on the day Charles Spurgeon showed up to church, but the "stupid man" seized the moment to preach his own simple message. That clumsy sermon to a handful of people in 1850 led to the conversion of a man who preached and wrote to untold thousands more. The impact of that message reverberates to this day, but the man had no idea what he had done. Pressed into service at the last minute because of an absent pastor, he simply spoke the truth he knew.

Or think of the priest who served Communion to Sara Miles. It was a routine ceremony on an ordinary day for most people at that church, but it was transformational for Miles. What about the person who baked the bread or prepared the wine? Could he or she have imagined what meaning would be drawn from those simple acts? Could George Buttrick have anticipated that a phrase he uttered that he hadn't even bothered to write down in the text of his sermon would draw a brilliant writer like Frederick Buechner into the kingdom of God? For those of us who are Christians, as we go about our lives we never know when we might be there at exactly the right moment to say or do the precise word or act that will light the way for someone to see Jesus.

Go to www.beaconhillbooks.com/go/godinpursuit for a free downloadable Study Guide that includes questions for deeper personal reflection as well as activities for use in a small-group setting.

THREE

Breaking Through to Faith
The Meaning of Conversion

Already we've seen that for many people, conversion to Christianity can be so inconvenient, so life-altering, at times even so life-threatening, that it's amazing it happens at all. But it does happen every day, and untold millions have experienced it. What combination of intellect, experience, revelation, emotion, and intervention of the Holy Spirit makes that turning point possible? What does "conversion" really mean? People encounter Jesus in radically different ways. Paul met Him amid light, blindness, and the Lord's audible voice on the Damascus road. Anne Lamott sensed Him hunkered down in the corner of her room. Charles Spurgeon found Him in a little church he wandered into because of a snowstorm. With so many different experiences, how can the concept of conversion be nailed down?

Inexpressible Joy: The Limitations of Language

To talk about conversion is immediately to run into the limitations of language. Our spiritual experiences shake us like nothing else, but how do we rise above inadequate expressions and clichés to express what they are really like? Saying that you are "saved" or "born again" or "converted" may be code words understood by others who have also encountered Christ, but they certainly don't fully capture the experience. Thomas Aquinas, philosopher and theologian and author of the classic *Summa Theologica*, had a spiritual encounter with Christ that was so profound it made him stop writing altogether. He said, "All that I have written seems to me like straw compared to what has now been revealed to me."

Theological concepts may be explained in precise language, but those technical terms do not capture the true experience any more than technically precise descriptions of music capture the joy of listening to it. Watch someone enjoying music on headphones. As the person bobs his or her head, dances around, squints, and lets slip an occasional grunt of sound, he or she may look and sound ridiculous. If you had never listened to music yourself, you might dismiss this person as deranged.

But because you've been moved by music yourself, you have some understanding of what he or she must be feeling, and if the music were released into the air for all to hear, you might even want to dance along with the person.

So it is with the power of the Holy Spirit. If you've sensed His presence, you know there's nothing else so deeply moving, but how could you ever adequately describe it?

Malcolm Muggeridge wrote that the "most characteristic and uplifting of the manifestations of conversion is rapture—an inexpressible joy which suffuses our whole being, making our fears dissolve into nothing, and our expectations move heavenwards." Even as great a writer as Muggeridge, however, does not know how to adequately describe that joy: "No earthly image can convey this adequately; music at its best—say, Mozart's *Exultate*—gets nearer to it than words."[1]

Years before her conversion, American writer, member of Congress, and ambassador Clare Booth Luce had a spiritual experience she did not understand at the time and that was hard to put into words. She wrote, "I expect the easiest thing is to say that suddenly SOMETHING WAS. My whole soul was cleft clean by it, as a silk veil slit by a shining sword. And I *knew*. I do not know now what I knew. I remember, I didn't know even then. That is, I didn't *know* with any 'faculty.'" Her whole nature "was adrift in this immense joy, as a speck of dust is seen to dance in a golden shaft of sunlight."[2] For months she marveled at the experience and reveled in it, and then gradually she forgot it.

The experience came back to her, years later, after her conversion, at the beginning of a service during prayers at the foot of the altar. At one point in the service an altar boy said, "Unto God, who giveth joy to my youth." The phrase had always awakened bitterness in Luce, because her own childhood had not been happy. But on this day the usual bitterness did not come when she heard those words. Instead, her experience by the ocean from years before flooded into her mind, and her heart "was gently suffused with an afterglow of that incredible joy."

It was not until then that she realized the experience from years before had played an enormous part in her conversion, even though she had seemed to forget it and could not explain exactly how it was connected. She writes, "I mention it here partly to elucidate the real difficulty of 'telling all' and partly lest anyone think the convert is not aware of the mysterious movements of his own soul, and that much of a conversion may take place on subconscious levels."[3]

Luce wisely points out that there may be more elements involved in conversion than we know or can tell. Many of us are able to look back on our conversion and pull out significant elements that become our "conversion story," but as with Clare Booth Luce and others we have looked at, there may be crucial factors—including the elements of "foreshadowing" discussed in the previous chapter—that may have led us to Christ in ways we're not fully aware of. Even parts of our experience that we *are* aware of, like Luce's experience at the ocean, can be hard to articulate in ways that capture the mysterious nature of what happened.

Lewis Rambo, who has studied conversion extensively and has identified seven stages in the process, stresses the *complexity* of conversion. He writes,

> As we have seen, conversion is a complex, multifaceted process involving personal, cultural, social, and religious dimensions. While conversion can be triggered by particular events and, in some cases, result in very sudden experiences of change, for the most part it takes place over a period of time. . . . Certain contemporary theologians believe that genuine conversion transpires over an entire lifetime.[4]

When Jesus spoke of conversion, His own ways of referring to it acknowledged its mysterious and ineffable but powerful nature. Throughout his teaching Jesus often used metaphors and parables rather than trying to nail down a concept in more direct theological terms. Look at the difficulty Nicodemus has with Jesus' way of speaking in John 3. When Jesus tells him that "no one can see the kingdom of God unless he is born again" (John 3:3), literal-minded Nicodemus thinks of physical birth and asks, "How can a man be born when he is old? Surely he cannot enter a second time into his mother's womb to be born!" (John 3:4). A few verses later, Jesus again evokes the power and mystery of how God works when He says, "The wind blows wherever it pleases. You hear its sound, but you cannot tell where it comes from or where it is going. So it is with everyone born of the Spirit" (John 3:8). Nicodemus' response: "How can this be?" (John 3:9).

Ways of Describing Conversion

None of this is to say that conversion can't be defined. The previous chapter considered Richard Peace's helpful explanation of conversion. He believes the essence of it can be found in Acts 26:18, in which the Lord tells Paul that He's sending him to the Gentiles "to open their eyes and turn them from darkness to light, and from the power of Satan to God, so that they may receive forgiveness of sins and a place among those who are sanctified by faith in me." The three elements of seeing ("open their eyes"), turning ("turn them from darkness to light"), and transformation ("that they may receive forgiveness of sins") are embodied in that scripture.

Gordon T. Smith defines conversion as "the human response to the saving work of God through Christ. Conversion is the initial encounter with God's saving grace—the steps or the means by which we enter into a redemptive relationship with God."[5] He describes seven elements that are involved in conversion. They're not consecutive steps, not hoops to be jumped through, but seven aspects of conversion that form a cluster of experience. They include (1) belief; (2) repentance; (3) trust and the assurance of forgiveness; (4) commitment, allegiance, and devotion; (5) water baptism; (6) reception of the gift of the Holy Spirit; and (7) incorporation into Christian community.[6]

Another scholar, D. G. Bloesch, explains that conversion is "both an event and a process. It signifies the action of the Holy Spirit upon us by which we are moved to respond to Jesus Christ in faith. It also includes the continuing work of the Holy Spirit within us purifying us in the image of Christ. This work of purification is accomplished as we repent and cling to Christ anew."[7]

The descriptions of the gospel message will certainly vary according to denominational and theological backgrounds. A Catholic would describe it differently than a Baptist. But some of the ways of conveying the essence of the Christian message do not contradict each other so much as they emphasize different aspects of the message. One of the more familiar ways of presenting the gospel is the Four Spiritual Laws, developed as a tract by Campus Crusade for Christ's Bill Bright. These four laws are "1. God loves you and offers a wonderful plan for your life. 2. All of us sin and our sin has separated us from God. 3. Jesus Christ is God's only provision for our sin. Through him we can know and experience God's love and plan for our life. 4. We must individually receive Jesus Christ as Savior and Lord; then we can know and experience God's love and plan for our lives."[8]

More recently, however, James Choung, a divisional director of InterVarsity Christian Fellowship in San Diego, has been using a different model to describe the Christian message to college students. He uses a diagram of four circles called the Big Story. The circles carry the phrases "Designed for good," "Damaged by evil," "Restored for better," and "Sent together to heal." These follow the biblical themes of creation, fall, redemption, and mission. As Choung explained in *Christianity Today*,

> As I'm drawing the four circles, I'll tell a story like this: The world, our relationships, and each of us were designed for good, but all of it was damaged by evil because of our self-centeredness and inclination to seek our own good above others'. But God loved the world too much to leave it that way, so he came as Jesus. He took everything evil with him to death on the cross, and through his resurrection, all of it was restored for better. In the end of time, all will be fully restored, but until then, the followers of Jesus are sent together to heal people, relationships, and the systems of the world.[9]

When people tell their own stories of salvation, as we'll see in upcoming chapters, some stress what they were converted *from*—purposelessness, sin, spiritual emptiness. Others emphasize what they are converted *to*—a relationship with Christ, joy, hope for eternity, the joy of being part of the community of fellow Christians.

Tim Stafford in his book *Surprised by Jesus* emphasizes Jesus' ushering in of the kingdom of God, which new believers can now take part in. He writes,

> Regardless of the audience, the basic summary of Jesus' "good news" stayed remarkably consistent. John had preached the same message: "Repent" (which means "turn in a new di-

rection"), "for the kingdom of God is near." By the time Paul wrote about that kingdom twenty-five years later, he could say, "the fulfillment of the ages has come" (1 Cor. 10:11). The kingdom of God is ongoing. . . .

If we want to follow Jesus' steps, we have to talk about an event. Call it the Jesus event. Jesus' life was the turning point in the history of Israel, in the history of the world and in the history of every human being. . . . When we preach the gospel, we announce what God has done to change the world. We offer our conviction that God is transforming the world and that each of us can take part in that transformation.[10]

Stafford emphasizes that salvation is not only for the individual inside a bubble. God is seeking to redeem all creation—individuals, families, societies, the whole world.

Differences and Patterns Within Conversions

Just as the limitations of language can skew our understanding of the breadth and depth of spiritual experience, so our own background with conversion may limit our grasp of the range of ways the transformation into Christianity takes place for different people.

In the church I grew up in, conversion happened in a certain way, and I saw little diversion from this pattern: it happened in church, at the altar that extended across the front of the sanctuary just in front of the pulpit. We knew, of course, that technically it was possible to turn to Christ without praying at an altar. People could accept Christ anywhere—at home, at school, at work. But those were exceptions. Ideally those places would have been equipped with an altar, but since they weren't, sometimes you had to make do. However, even those more impromptu conversions often would be followed by a symbolic trip to the altar at the end of the next Sunday service.

The usual process for conversion at our Nazarene church was this: you show up at church as a nonbeliever, and you might spend a few Sundays—or weeks or months—learning about the gospel in sermons and songs and Sunday school classes. Eventually you feel the tug of the Holy Spirit drawing you toward Him and convincing you of your need for salvation. This pull is called "conviction" or "conviction of sin," and it is a call to repentance, forgiveness, and relationship with Jesus Christ. At the end of a church service, after the singing, prayer, and sermon, the pastor gives an invitation for anyone who wants to receive Christ to come to the altar to pray. The pastor might model for the would-be convert the prayer of repentance of sins and the seeking of forgiveness.

Then it's decision time. As music plays and everyone waits, those who want to pray step out to the altar and do so. Christians may surround the person and join in the prayer. The seeker prays the prayer, the Holy Spirit enters into the life of the person, and conversion is complete. Baptism would follow at some point, but in our tradition there was no particular hurry about it. The conversion was what happened at the altar, and baptism was an important public sign of it.

This is how I came to Christ, and while growing up I saw hundreds of others come to Him in the same way over the years. It's a beautiful way and is still the standard practice in many churches. Stepping out from the pew toward the altar is a powerful spiritual, psychological, and physical step toward belief. It's also a public step, taking conversion beyond what could become merely a vague back-and-forth internal deliberation and making it an event. It establishes a definite time and place when you say, "Here is where I confess my sins and ask for forgiveness, and here is where I declare my intention to be a follower of Jesus Christ." It allows brothers and sisters in Christ to gather round you in support. You're joining the Body of Christ. The church knows it and can follow up and help you become a disciple as you grow in your faith.

It's a good way—but it accounts for surprisingly few of the conversions I studied. It doesn't account for Paul's conversion on the way to Damascus. It doesn't account for C. S. Lewis's conversion on the way to the zoo, or Mary Kay Beard's conversion in prison, or Linda Freeman's in a dorm room, or the conversions of Lauren Winner and others that happened so gradually that they can't identify a time and place.

The circumstances of conversion vary greatly, and so do the tipping points that lead up to that crucial moment. But in my interviews with Christians and my research of spiritual memoirs, I found five tipping points into faith that emerged more often than any others. The following chapters will illustrate some of the surprising and inspiring ways those tipping points worked to usher people into the presence of Jesus Christ.

Go to www.beaconhillbooks.com/go/godinpursuit for a free downloadable Study Guide that includes questions for deeper personal reflection as well as activities for use in a small-group setting.

FOUR

Tipping Point 1
When God Finds You at Your Lowest Point

To be a rock star.

You're drowning in millions of dollars. You can buy anything you want. You travel the world. You're adored by screaming fans. You make music you love and know that people are enjoying it in their homes and cars and everywhere that some electronic device can pump it into their heads.

For some it's the ultimate fantasy. They would give or do *any-thing* to achieve such a dream.

Brian Welch, lead guitarist for the phenomenally successful rock group Korn, was one of the few who made it. By 2004 he had experienced years of wealth, fame, and every pleasure he could imagine. Where did it leave him? In his memoir he writes, "Here I was, the guitarist for one of the biggest rock bands in the world, raking in millions of bucks and playing huge concerts all over the globe, but I was completely miserable. I didn't understand how a person who had everything he wanted, with millions of dollars in the bank, could be unhappy."

In spite of his outward success, Welch had reached the lowest point of his life. What was his response? He says, "The thought of this made me so depressed that I turned to the only thing I knew that could comfort me: drugs. That year, I pretty much lived on beer, pills, speed, and peanut butter and jelly sandwiches. Part of me wanted to get cleaned up, but another part of me wanted to die from a drug overdose."[1] Was there any way out of his dilemma short of self-destruction?

Money, Fame, and Agony

Joe Eszterhas also achieved a level of success that some would sell their souls for. As the screenwriter of such films as *Jagged Edge*, *Basic Instinct*, *Flashdance*, and *Showgirls*, Eszterhas had made millions and was a person of power in Hollywood.

Then his life fell apart. Only weeks after he and his family moved from Malibu to Ohio so that his children could grow up in a more traditional atmosphere than Hollywood, he was diagnosed with throat cancer and had eighty percent of his larynx removed. He was told to stop smoking and drinking or he would die. He had been smoking since he was twelve years old and was also a long-time heavy drinker. He didn't think he could stop, but he tried.

The lowest point came after about a month of no smoking or drinking. He was going crazy—twitching, trembling, and yelling at his family. He left the house to take a walk. He explained, "I was trying to outwalk my cravings and my addictions. I was trying to outwalk panic. I was trying to outwalk my own self-destructiveness. I was trying to outwalk death."

The walk that hot afternoon was agony. He was hot, he was sweating, he was shaking, he couldn't breathe. He says, "I started to cry. I was hyperventilating. I sat down on the curb. Tears were streaming down my face. I watched them splatter on the ground. My heart hammered so loudly, it blocked everything out except my sobs. I didn't sound human to myself. I listened to myself moaning. I sounded like a wounded animal."[2]

At that moment, his fabulous Hollywood success—the influence, the money—offered nothing to release him from the crisis that he expected might kill him. Where would help come from?

What It Takes to Wake Us Up

For these two men and countless other people, the tipping point from disbelief into faith in Christ happens when everything safe and pleasant is swept away and is replaced by meaninglessness or suffering. It may be reaching the low point of a career. It may be the destruction of a marriage. It may be unjust treatment. It may be the tragic and unexpected loss of a loved one. It may be devastating illness. Even if the person outwardly still appears to be on top, the crisis might be the disillusioning sense of meaninglessness of that "success."

Like the other tipping points into faith, reaching this crisis can cause a person to tip either way, either toward faith in God or toward bitterness, deeper disbelief, depression, even suicide. Sometimes at this moment, with all other options for fulfillment revealed as falsehoods, people turn to God and find spiritual rescue. For them the suffering serves the function of waking them up to spiritual reality. Backed into a corner, they have to ask, what matters? What can I ultimately count on? What lasts? What is real?

For most of us it's easier to be spiritually asleep than awake. Walk through the shopping mall or go to a restaurant or even stand in the church foyer and listen to what people are talking about. Rarely do the discussions turn to crucially important spiritual questions: Why am I here? What happens after death? What is the truth about Jesus Christ? In many social situations, bringing up such topics would be considered rude. Like politics or other sensitive topics, it's best to stay away from them.

Better to skim the surface of life, do whatever it takes to avoid pain, and maximize the good times. Keep the focus on more day-to-day concerns—getting the bills paid, taking care of the family, having some fun, achieving success, avoiding disaster, doing the laundry, making the meal, watching the TV show.

Some people *choose* to live in a spiritual daze, and others do so without realizing it. It's easy to put off thinking about the big spiritual questions for a long time. It may even seem morbid to focus on the fact that you eventually will grow old and die, that everyone you love will die, that everything you own will eventually crumble to dust, that you will face sickness, loss, disappointments. You do everything possible to keep such thoughts at a distance. You build and plan and live as if the good life will go on forever.

Some people avoid these questions their entire lives and head into eternity not knowing or not thinking that answers to such questions are even possible. But for some, when hard times force such questions into their lives, they find, as did the reluctant converts discussed in previous chapters, that God is already headed toward them, present in their pain, redeeming it, waiting to save them.

When Success Is Not Enough

Some people believe they have not achieved fulfillment because they have not yet reached the heights of wealth, power, and fame that would validate them. Rock star Brian Welch and screenwriter Joe Eszterhas achieved all those things but "woke up" to find that their lives were still a miserable mess and that neither wealth nor fame nor drugs nor drinking offered them any true escape from their dilemma.

To their tremendous surprise, that is when God arrived.

Although Brian Welch would eventually get about as far from God as it was possible to go, early on he had an experience that foreshadowed his eventual turn to Jesus Christ. Although he was from an unreligious family, when he was thirteen a friend's mother told him about Jesus, and Brian decided to ask Jesus to come into his heart. He knelt on the floor alone and did so. He says that even though he "felt something inside me change," he didn't know what to do about it. His "knees were getting cold from the tile, so I got up and pretty much went on with my life. I didn't know it at the time, but something had been set in motion in my life, something that I wouldn't experience for another twenty years or so."[3]

Those next twenty years were filled with astonishing success in music, copious drug use, a difficult and abusive and ultimately failed marriage, and finally complete disillusionment with all his life had become. Jesus came back into Brian's life through his relationship with two friends who worked with him on his real estate investments. One day when Brian was at a low point, out of nowhere he received an e-mail from his friend Eric that read, "Not to get weird on you or anything, but I was reading my Bible this morning, and you came to mind when I read this verse." The verse was Matthew 11:28-29—"Come to me, all you who are weary and burdened, and I will give you rest. Take my yoke upon you and learn from me, for I am gentle and humble in heart, and you will find rest for your souls."

That message triggered an e-mail exchange and a series of other events that all conspired to wake up Brian Welch to the fact that God was pursuing him. He writes, "Everywhere I went, I ran into someone who wanted to bring up Jesus—it was becoming inescapable." Old friends he used to do drugs with but hadn't seen in years reemerged in his life and now were Christians. People kept inviting him to church. Eventually he went to church with one of his friends, and there on the screen was the same Matthew 11:28-29 scripture that Eric had e-mailed him weeks earlier. He thought Eric must have set him up by telling the pastor to use that scripture, but he hadn't. Brian started seeing that scripture everywhere over the next few weeks. God was calling him.

A battle raged within him. He writes, "I had so much hope, but it quickly faded away when I thought about being a Christian. *You don't want to turn into one of those geeky people you see on the Christian channel on TV, I thought. Everyone would laugh at you. Don't be an idiot.* But then I had other thoughts that went the other direction. *What, are you going to stay in Korn, stay hooked on drugs, and die? You going to leave your kid fatherless?*[4]

Brian Welch finally became a Christian, but it was not an instantaneous or easy turn. He would pray and then relapse into drugs. He sensed God telling him to quit Korn, and he did so. He stayed on the tipping point for a while, sometimes tipping one way, sometimes another. In the end, he chose to believe the message from Matthew 11 that had pursued him, and in Jesus Christ he found rest for his soul.

Saved? Who, Me? From What?

The crisis for Joe Eszterhas was even more immediate. His turn to God was also more sudden and more of a shock to him.

That day as he sat sobbing and moaning on the sidewalk in intense pain, barely able to breathe, he heard himself mumble something that he couldn't believe he was saying: "Please, God—help me."

In his memoir he wrote, "I was praying. Asking. Begging. For help. Begging God to help me. And I thought, *Me? Asking God? Begging* God? Praying? I hadn't even thought about God since I was a boy, yet I was listening to myself begging Him for help over and over and over again as I moaned in pain."

Then his heart calmed, the shaking stopped, and he was able to stand. He saw "a shimmering, dazzling, nearly blinding brightness that made me cover my eyes with my hands." The brightness faded, and he walked home. "Something happened to me on that hellish muggy day as I sat on the curb seven years ago. For a long time I didn't know how to describe what it was, but now I do. *I was saved.*"

The term "saved" was hard for Eszterhas to come to terms with. Someone had to suggest to him that being saved is what happened to him that day. For many years he had mocked conversion and made fun of Christians. He had taught his children that God was an irrelevant concept. But now he knew that this is what had happened to him. What was he saved from? "From the darkness that I had been drawn to most of my life, the evil I had spent so much time and effort studying and analyzing from the time I was a young man."[5]

It was evil he had made millions writing about, but now it was no longer in control of him. In spite of the derision and difficulty his new faith would bring him from some of the people who had known him before, Joe Eszterhas was now a Christian.

Illness as a Path to Spiritual Renewal

One of the most common low points in life that serves as a tipping point toward or away from faith is severe illness. Joe Eszterhas came to grips with his need for God only when his body gave out and he had to look beyond himself for meaning and salvation.

About 250 years earlier, a young man who would become a great Quaker leader and writer went through his own battle with illness that helped tip him into faith in Jesus Christ.

John Woolman "began to be acquainted with the operations of divine love" even before age seven, and he felt drawn to read scripture and think on heavenly things while other children played. As he grew up he drifted from Christ, and serious reflection became uneasy for him.

Then he got sick. It was not some ordinary, inconvenient childhood illness. This was a sickness so severe that it made him wish he had never been born. As he later wrote, it got so bad that he

> doubted of recovery; then did darkness, horror, and amazement with full force seize me, even when my pain and distress of body were very great. I thought it would have been better for me never to have had being, than to see the day which I now saw. I was filled with confusion, and in great affliction, both of mind and body, I lay and bewailed myself.

With his being in such a state, you might think that Woolman would have been so focused on his physical suffering that he would set aside spiritual questions until he could concentrate on them better. At first, sensing the estrangement from God that had characterized his life leading up to the illness, he did not have the confidence to cry out for help. But finally, like Eszterhas gasping for breath on the sidewalk, Woolman's concerns were narrowed to such essential realities that he couldn't help but contemplate his relationship to God. He says that, humbled before the Lord, he turned to Him for mercy and spiritual renewal:

> At length that word which is a fire and a hammer broke and dissolved my rebellious heart; my cries were put up in contrition; and in the multitude of his mercies I found inward relief, and a close engagement that if he was pleased to restore my health I might walk humbly before him.[6]

God did restore Woolman's health, and though this event did not end Woolman's spiritual struggles, it was an important turning point toward the Lord. He went on to become, among other things, an outspoken and influential advocate for abolishing slavery.

Jeff Friend's movement toward a true relationship with Jesus Christ was triggered by a physical problem he at first thought was tiny. He thought the bump just above his right ankle was a mosquito bite. It wouldn't stop itching, but he expected it to go away. Instead, the bump flattened out and grew bigger. He went to the doctor, but none of the prescribed remedies worked.

The wound became five inches long, three inches wide, and the "pain was indescribable," said Friend. "Every step I took on that leg was agonizing." A surgeon eventually concluded that Jeff had been bitten by a brown recluse spider.

But even after two years of treatments and surgeries, the doctors couldn't find a way to heal Jeff's leg. "I was as low as I had ever been, in extreme physical pain and depressed by the lack of medical success." His marriage was also in trouble. He writes, "God had brought me to the place where I had to face myself."

Friend had always presented himself as a Christian. He was a churchgoing man. But now that his world was "in shambles," he decided to face the truth. He made an appointment with his wife to go visit a pastor. He told the pastor, "Everybody would tell you that I'm a Christian, but it's all a lie—every bit of it. I've never accepted Jesus as my Savior."[7] That day Jeff prayed authentically and became a Christian.

His physical healing was still several years away, he was still in constant pain—but spiritually, the crisis had jolted him out of the complacent lies in which he had drifted for years, and now he was an authentic disciple of Jesus.

Spiritual Enlightenment Through Physical Danger

For all the persons discussed in this chapter so far, an unexpected and unwanted jolt brought them to their senses and allowed them to consider where they stood spiritually and what part they wanted God to play in their lives. For John Newton, who would become best known for writing "Amazing Grace" and almost three hundred other hymns, the jolt came in the form of a ship that almost sank.

Newton first went to sea at age eleven and worked his way up to become captain of a British slave ship. On one sea voyage, before he was a captain, Newton was awakened at night by violent waves that flooded his cabin and that brought the cry from deck that the ship was sinking. As Newton helped in the fight to save the craft, one of the crew members was swept overboard, and the upper timbers of one side of the ship were torn away. Newton later wrote, "Taking in all circumstances, it was astonishing, and almost miraculous, that any of us survived to relate the story."

All night the crew battled to save the ship. They plugged up leaks with their clothes and bedding. By nine o'clock in the morning the struggle was still far from over, and Newton went to speak to the captain for a moment. When that conversation ended and he returned to his post, Newton said out loud, "If this will not do, the Lord have mercy upon us." Newton later wrote, "This (though spoken with little reflection) was the first desire I had breathed for mercy for the space of many years."

Newton's "prayer" was so perfunctory and, by his own admission, uttered with so little depth of thought that it sounds too trivial to count as a turning point toward conversion to Christ. But as with the prodigal son, even the smallest turn toward the Father brings the loving God running toward him. Newton had started on his path to Jesus.

First, however, he had to survive the storm, and that looked unlikely. He still had more hours of pumping to do to save the ship, with "almost every wave breaking over my head." Beyond the physical danger, Newton was now awakened to his own spiritual danger:

> Indeed, I expected that every time the vessel descended in the sea, she would rise no more; and though I dreaded death now, and my heart foreboded the worst, if the scriptures, which I had long since opposed, were indeed true; yet still I was but half convinced, and remained for a space of time in a sullen frame, a mixture of despair and impatience. I thought, if the Christian religion was true, I could not be forgiven; and was, therefore, expecting, and almost at time, wishing, to know the worst of it.[8]

Newton did not suffer "the worst of it," either physically or spiritually. He survived the ship disaster, and then, for "the space of about six years, the Lord was pleased to lead me in a secret way." Newton understood sin and his own evil. He had read the Bible many times and knew the basic tenets of Christianity. But his ideas were confused, and he had no one to guide him. He prayed for someone to guide him, and God answered that prayer with a Christian friend who led him farther down the path of discipleship.

With the help of his friend, Newton "began to understand the security of the covenant of grace, and to expect to be preserved, not by my own power and holiness, but by the mighty power and promise of God, through faith in an unchangeable Savior."[9] He went on to leave the slave trade, become a preacher, and write one of the most famous hymns in history. Like Woolman, he also became a strong anti-slavery spokesman. But the turning point was one tiny movement toward God in a panic-stricken moment.

When Injustice Obliterates Pride

One of the reasons the illnesses and career disillusionments and physical disasters related in this chapter act as tipping points toward faith is that they break people out of their sense of self-sufficiency. Pride—the idea that I'm fine on my own and don't really need God—is one of the biggest barriers to faith. A crisis can lead to the tough realization that no matter how self-contained we think we are, the fact is we're frail human beings entirely dependent on God for every moment of our existence. Self-sufficiency is a dangerous illusion.

Ninoy Aquino was a powerful Philippine politician in 1972 when Dictator Ferdinand Marcos arrested him and thousands of others and locked him away in prison during the imposition of martial law. As Gordon T. Smith tells the story, Aquino was first held in a cubicle in a bungalow at a military camp and was later transferred to another military fort, where he was held in a tiny cell. He was given little food and was held in solitary confinement for a month, with only underclothes to wear.

Alone and tormented, his future bleak, he seethed with anger and frustration. Why should a dictator like Marcos get away with living a life of splendor and treating people like garbage while a good man like Aquino rotted away in his underwear in a tiny cell? Aquino complained loudly to God. But then in the midst of his bitterness toward God, he heard a voice that said, "Why do you cry?

I have gifted you with consolations, honors and glory which have been denied to millions of your countrymen. Now that I visit you with a slight desolation, you cry and whimper like a spoiled brat."

Pretty harsh, but Aquino's pride had been swept aside. Only the deeper, essential issues remained. He "fell to his knees, asked for forgiveness and chose to give his life to the service of God, then 'picked up my cross and followed Him.'" In his suffering Aquino realized that "pride had blinded him to the presence of God in his life—the same pride that had fostered a love of temporal power, honors, and joys. In the end he saw something providential even in the persecution of a dictator: 'If only for my conversion, I should owe the tyrant my eternal gratitude.'"[10] Aquino was grateful to a dictator, not for unjust imprisonment but for unintentionally awakening him to what really matters.

Go to www.beaconhillbooks.com/go/godinpursuit for a free downloadable Study Guide that includes questions for deeper personal reflection as well as activities for use in a small-group setting.

FIVE

Tipping Point 2
When Circumstances and a
Spiritual Messenger Conspire

Linda Freeman was a 19-year-old college student, minding her own business and not seeking spiritual guidance, when she began having strange encounters regarding Jesus at every turn. When she stepped outside the library at Duquesne University to take a cigarette break, she noticed a man walking up the hill. She didn't know him, wanted nothing to do with him, and looked off in a different direction. A moment later he stood in front of her and asked, "Do you know why Jesus died?"

Trying to buy time to figure out how to deal with this guy, she looked down at the ground and stubbed out her cigarette. The man didn't say anything else, and when Linda looked up to answer him, he was gone. It was not just that he was walking away from her—he was nowhere to be seen.

She put the incident out of her mind until a few days later when she went downtown to buy a few things at the drugstore. On a sidewalk crowded with lunch-hour pedestrians, a stranger emerged from the crowd, looked right into her face, and asked, "If you died today, do you know if you would go to heaven?"

65

Too surprised to know how to respond, Linda fiddled with the packages in her arms for a moment and ignored him. Surprise quickly turned to annoyance, and she looked up to tell him to get out of her face. He had already melted into the crowd. Two important but irritating spiritual questions flung at her by two strangers. What did it mean? She decided not to let it upset her. But the questions, and the weird way they came to her, would not leave her mind.

Linda decided to find a way to either dismiss the questions or answer them. She said, "I had been a hard-partying girl since junior high school, but I was also an excellent student with good grades throughout high school and now college. I'd always relied on my intelligence and resourcefulness to meet every challenge. I argued with myself that I was a good person, completely happy with myself and my life and that there wasn't anything 'wrong' with me."[1]

Still, that self-justification didn't exactly answer the questions that had been put to her, so she sought answers on her own. She sat down and started reading the Bible. The effort was a failure. The book made no sense. "It might as well have been written in Mandarin Chinese," she said. "I'd been a voracious reader all my life and couldn't ever recall not being able to understand whatever I read on some level. But I had to give up on the Bible approach to finding answers to the two questions that now seemed to torment me."

She browsed through a few "God books" in the library, but they were no help either. She decided to abandon this spiritual quest. She had hoped to have an answer for any other weirdo who might approach her about Jesus, but after all, what were the chances it would happen a third time?

It did happen. A week later, at four in the morning, Linda and several friends sat at McDonald's "already hung over from the previous night's partying but trying to catch our second wind." The place was packed with weekend partiers, but then two very sober young men entered, one with a large book under his arm. Linda immediately sensed that she was about to have another inexplicable encounter.

"See those two guys over there who just walked in?" she asked her friends. "They're going to walk right up to me and ask me some weird questions about religion or God and then walk away. Just watch."

Linda said her friends "looked at me as though I suffered from some sort of alcohol-related delusion," but the two guys walked directly over to her, and the one with the book asked, "Have you asked Jesus into your heart?"

She didn't even try to answer, and the men didn't wait for a response. They turned and walked out the door. "My friends were completely freaked out. They were even more freaked out when I told them the whole story. Sadly, not one of them had a clue how to answer these questions either."

Linda couldn't get the questions out of her mind; she didn't know how to answer them. She wanted to find answers not so much for her own spiritual benefit but so she could be prepared with a response that would "make these guys go away and stop bothering me." The following Sunday evening, as she played cards with friends in her dorm, she had trouble concentrating and folded her hand and quit. That's when it hit her. She could ask David, a Christian acquaintance who lived in her dorm. If anyone knew the answers to the three questions, he would. She rushed to his room.

As soon as the surprised young man answered the door, she blurted out, "I need to know why Jesus died, how to know if I'm going to heaven, and what it means to ask Jesus into my heart. If you know the answers to these questions, I really need you to tell them to me."

Linda says, "Looking back, I have to laugh when I think of this moment. Can you imagine being a born-again, committed Christian, living in the midst of all these hardcore partying coeds and no doubt praying for them all to be saved, and one of the worst of the bunch shows up at your door and says she absolutely must have the answers to the three key questions for salvation? Needless to say, David invited me in."

David told her the gospel message, but he was not the only one speaking to her. The Holy Spirit also was moving within her. "As David's mouth continued to move, something began happening inside of me. I started to feel a presence and a power and a peace that I'd never ever known before. I became overwhelmed by whatever it was and all I knew was that I wanted more." Linda became a Christian that night. "As David led me through the simple prayer that I later learned is called 'the sinner's prayer,' I knew that I had literally come face-to-face with the risen, living Lord Jesus Christ. It was absolutely unbelievable. It was as though the heavens had opened and He was standing there right in front of me."

The Surprising Role of the Spiritual Messenger

One thing I've learned by listening to and studying dozens of conversion stories is that becoming a Christian is rarely a solitary event. Even people who are alone at the actual moment of conversion almost never reached that moment on their own but were led there in various ways by others whom the Lord seems to have carefully placed along the way.

If someone asked who led me to Christ, I might first think of my pastor, since he preached the sermon that I responded to when I gave my life to Christ. But I've also already mentioned the woman who welcomed me into that church the first day I visited there, and my uncle who invited me. And then there were my parents who continued to take me to that church, the people in the bus ministry who sometimes picked me up for Sunday School, the Sunday School teachers who taught me, friends who were already Christians, and many others too numerous to mention. In a sense, they all served as spiritual guides or messengers since each led me a little closer to Jesus Christ.

Those who help lead others to Christ could be called by many names—"witnesses," "advocates," "mentors"—but in this chapter I'll refer to them as spiritual messengers. While nearly every conversion includes such people, there are some conversions, such as Linda Freeman's, in which the spiritual messengers play a particular role at the tipping point into faith. Sometimes these messengers are friends who actually present the gospel message, such as David in Linda's story. Sometimes they're strangers who play one specific role and then disappear, such as the people who kept popping up and asking Linda bothersome spiritual questions.

Repeatedly I've seen examples in which God appears to have conspired to place His messengers at just the right place and just the right time to lead people to an encounter with Him.

The Spiritual Messenger as Conspirator

I'm not surprised that people need the help of a spiritual guide as they contemplate becoming Christians. The surprising part is the role that these messengers actually play—and do not play—at the point of conversion.

Here's the pattern I would expect played out in an example: A woman finds her interest sparked in Christianity for some reason. She begins to investigate it. She visits a church. She talks to people she trusts who happen to be Christians. One of those Christians emerges as a guide to answer her questions and to lead her to books and experts who will give her a solid education in theology and satisfy any objections that might occur to her. Once this process is complete and the nonbeliever is ready to move forward, the guide can lead her in the prayer of conversion. Afterward, the guide can continue to help her as she moves forward in Christian discipleship.

Sometimes the process happens that way, but most of the time it doesn't. Most of the time those various roles are filled not by one person but by several. And even though the various messengers may be unaware of each other, they play their parts in a way that makes it look as if someone had designed the whole thing.

Myles Weiss was a Jewish man knowledgeable in his faith who fell for a vivacious and outspoken Christian young woman. Although he was attracted to nearly everything about her, her unswerving devotion to Christ unnerved him. He writes, "She was a challenge. She had morals. And she challenged me, as in 'I dare you to be intellectually honest and study the Hebrew Scriptures to see if Jesus is the Messiah!'"

Weiss decided to meet her challenge by reversing it on her and awakening her to "the deeper things of spiritual life." He also prayed for guidance.

That guidance came the next day in the form of a stranger, a man in the parking lot of the local college where Myles was waiting to attend class. The man was a musician, and he and Myles talked music as they listened to the stereo of Myles' new red sports car. The stranger said something completely unexpected: "You know, the real reason I came over here is that the Lord told me to go talk to the guy with the red car. You've been praying for guidance."

How could this stranger possibly have known about Myles' prayer for guidance? The man went on to tell Myles that there was a battle for his soul and that Jesus wanted Myles to know Him. Weiss writes, "I stood and stared. I tried to excuse myself, wanting to escape from this zealot. . . . I was in awe, quite spooked . . . and ready for something familiar. But the 'familiar' patterns of my life were about to change forever."[2]

The stranger, whose name was James, handed Myles a tape of his Christian band's music and asked to listen to it on Myles' car stereo. They tried to insert it, but the old tape wouldn't eject. The car was brand new, and the stereo had never malfunctioned. James told Myles the enemy of his soul didn't want him to hear songs about Jesus, the Messiah. Myles's reaction: "I wanted to run."

They finally got the old tape out. "My tape was bent, as if it had been melted, which seemed impossible." James told him, "The devil is real, and he'll resist your turning to Jesus. Don't worry, though. Jesus is stronger and will help you if you ask Him." Myles left with a reluctant promise to meet with James again. He went straight to

Alison. "I wanted to tell her that her spiritual Master had sent an emissary to mess with me. The 'messing' had begun."

Over the next several weeks "inexplicable experiences melded with Scripture" to finally convince Myles of who Jesus is. He became a Christian, and he also married Alison. James and Alison each served indispensable roles as messengers in Myles's journey toward Christ. If Alison had not been in his life, urging him closer to Christ, Myles might have easily dismissed James as a kook. But without James's confirmation of some of the things Alison had been telling him, Myles might have remained stuck in his skepticism indefinitely. Even though James and Alison didn't know each other, they conspired as messengers to bring the gospel to one who became a new believer.

Spiritual Messengers May Not Know the Significance of Their Actions

With multiple spiritual messengers often acting in someone's life at the same time, the messengers may be unaware of the part they're playing in leading someone to Christ. They may think their actions are insignificant, but those words or deeds may enter someone's life at just the right moment to have an enormous impact.

When Mary Adele LaClair was "investigating" Jesus, she had an encounter that could have gone very wrong but instead ushered her into a new relationship with God. One day as Mary stood crying in her living room, putting away her cot for the day, she demanded of God, *When will I have suffered enough to pay for my sins?*

Never was the answer she sensed.

At first she felt hopelessly lost, but the answer did not satisfy her. She was not a Christian, but she had been brought up in church and parochial school and knew about Jesus. She believed there must be some hope in Him, and she decided to investigate Him. Mary says that once she made that decision, "at once the air in the room became lighter. A breath of fresh air came into the room, and the same breath of fresh air entered my spirit."[3]

Mary told God it was "up to Him to lead me to the truth without any sidetracks." She was at a delicate point in her spiritual journey, and her faith could have tipped either way. But life does not come to a standstill during a spiritual crisis, and Mary's next problem was of a more practical kind. She moved into a new apartment, and her dog got into a "vicious, victorious dog fight" with two other dogs. The two defeated dogs belonged to her neighbor, and the neighbor came knocking on Mary's door.

Already under stress with many problems, Mary thought, *How much more can I take?* As she approached the door, she agonized. *I'll probably wind up in jail, or maybe she's going to sue me.*

Mary could not have been more surprised by the words her neighbor spoke: "Do you want to come pray with us?"

Mary was wary of this offer, knowing what had happened with the dogs. But she reminded herself that she had asked God to lead her, so she reluctantly went with her new neighbor to join a group in prayer, Bible reading, and singing. God was indeed pursuing her, and after more prayer and several more meetings, Mary said she "prayed to the risen Jesus, asked Him into my heart, and received the baptism in the Holy Spirit."

Mary's neighbor had arrived in her life at exactly the right moment, and instead of pressing a grievance about a dog fight, she chose to be a messenger of the gospel instead.

When Messengers Aren't Delivering the Message They Intend

Not only are spiritual messengers sometimes unaware of the significance of their actions and their place in someone's story, but they also sometimes aren't even sending the message they intend. In some cases God uses messengers who aren't Christians to get through to someone when the Christian witnesses have failed.

As a 21-year-old student at a Christian college, Tom Allbaugh decided he no longer wanted to serve God and wasn't even sure he still believed in Him. Many factors led to his decision. He also was troubled by difficult intellectual questions about Christianity, such as why evil exists in a world created by a good, sovereign, loving God. No single issue pushed him away from the Lord, but gradually he simply came to believe that what his agnostic father believed about religion was true. He didn't want to be a hypocrite. He stopped calling himself a Christian.

Over the next seven years he continued sliding into cynicism, not only toward Christianity but also toward much of the rest of life as well. His sister's death in a car accident deepened his sense of hopelessness. He felt guilt over her death because he had introduced her to her husband, who drove the car. The husband was a person who, if Tom had still been a Christian, he would not have introduced his sister to.

Tom said that "three months before her death, I had a dream that she was killed, and her death would be on my hands. I woke up from that dream with a vivid sense of the spiritual dimension of the universe, but I didn't know what to do about it." By age 29, in graduate school, stalled in his studies, and bouncing around among a series of unsatisfying jobs, he called himself a "true cynic" who had "learned to see the hollowness of everything."

The turning points were slow and tentative. One of his professors, seeing Tom's unhappiness in a dead-end, part-time job, asked, "Doesn't it kill your spirit?"

It was a casual comment, perhaps, but it made Tom think. "I never had a college professor, even at the religious institution where I studied in the seventies, refer to the spirit in such personal terms, but especially to my spirit as a reality, as something that could be enhanced, emboldened, expanded, or deadened by daily living."[4]

At this same time Tom started rooming with some Christian students, not because he desired Christian roommates but because it was an economic necessity. He didn't want to have much to do with them. They talked about their faith but in ways that turned him off to Christianity even more. They talked more about Satan than God, and to Tom,

> this seemed about as childish and stupid as anything I might hear. . . . I didn't stop to analyze their theology because it seemed all too typical: Talk to the unsaved about the bad guy, about the exciting, evil stuff. After you've described in vivid detail the nasty arsonist and the house he's set on fire, show the little fire escape he calls God.

Tom wasn't buying any of it, and his familiarity with Christian culture and language made him even more resistant than someone who had never heard the gospel. "This was the evangelical shtick," he said. "I'd seen it all at this point. The trouble with talking like that to someone as burned out and calloused as me is I'd seen this approach from both sides. I was once over there. I'd read some theology, and I didn't know why this person was talking to me as though I was a high school student."

Up to this point it's hard to imagine a less promising potential convert to Christianity. Everything—especially the verbiage coming from Christians themselves—seemed to be pushing Tom farther away from Christ rather than closer to Him. However, other forces were at work inside him. Even though he rejected his roommate's simplistic notions about God and Satan, he was attracted by the fact that, like the professor who asked about his spirit, his roommate at least seemed to be aware that a spiritual realm existed.

Tom thought, *No one else has been talking like this. No one else acts as though the world is bigger than the sky, the earth, the sun. No one else thinks that there's more to life than the material.*

Although Tom had basically accepted this materialistic philosophy for seven years, he increasingly had his doubts about it.

> I suddenly had insomnia in my girlfriend's apartment. I got up, found a Bible, and sat in the living room at three-thirty in

the morning reading from the Psalms and fearing that there *was* more to life than chemicals, and I had missed the boat. I was lost eternally. I had walked away from knowing God, and there was nothing that could help me. I had experienced, like everyone else, I think, a range of light and darkness. The light I once knew made this darkness especially flattening and uncreative. I felt myself in danger of losing who I was.

Eventually, doubts about his own unbelief and weariness with being bound up in materialistic despair brought Tom to a place where he was ready to believe in Jesus Christ again. But he couldn't quite bring himself to take the final step into faith. He needed something to help usher him back into belief, and that something came in the form of an unusual spiritual messenger.

One night a stranger approached Tom and asked to pray with him. The man spoke about what he sensed was trouble in Tom's life, and he wanted him to know that the Lord's compassion was great. This man could not have known of the burden Tom carried about his sister, but the words struck him deeply. A year or two earlier, such a request for prayer from a stranger—or any other Christian for that matter—would have been met with a scornful response.

Even now, open as he was to belief, Tom didn't exactly embrace the man. He says,

> I've since decided that the shrug of my shoulder that night and my sort of noncommittal "might as well, whatever" was good enough for God to accept as a step toward Him, for the stranger began to speak into my life concerning things it was impossible for him to know. By the end of the prayer, I was kneeling in belief, giving my life over to Christ and His way, warmed beyond any earthly warmth with His love and compassion for me.

What If the Spiritual Messenger Fails to Deliver the Message?

Although there are many inspiring stories of people who move into faith in Jesus with the help of spiritual messengers who enter their lives at just the right moment, I also found a disturbing number of stories in which the messengers were *not* there when people needed them most. These failures led to spiritual confusion and lost opportunities to help people move into true and deeper faith.

E. Stanley Jones became an influential Christian speaker, missionary, and writer, but his true conversion was delayed for lack of a spiritual guide. At the end of a sermon one day, a guest preacher pointed to the fifteen-year-old Jones and a group of his friends in the gallery of the church and said, "Young men, Jesus said, 'He that is not with me is against me.'" Jones was moved. He decided to give himself to Christ. None of his friends wanted to go down to the altar with him, so he climbed over his friends, walked down to the altar alone, and knelt there. He was sincere in his desire to meet Christ, but he needed someone to help show him how. He needed guidance. He needed the spiritual mentor who was not there.

He says, "I felt undone and wept—wept because I was guilty and estranged. I fumbled for the latchstring of the Kingdom of God, missed it, for they didn't tell me the steps to find. . . . I wanted the Kingdom of God, wanted reconciliation with my Heavenly Father, but took church membership as a substitute."

Conversion did not happen that day for Jones. He "felt religious for a few weeks, and then it all faded out and I was back again exactly where I was before. . . . I was outwardly in, but not inwardly in. It was a sorry impasse. I could have lived out my life on that level the balance of my days, a cancelled-out person, neither here nor there."[5]

Unfortunately, many people do live their entire spiritual lives at that "in-between" place, settling for a pale imitation of Christian faith rather than enjoying the true joy of a real relationship with Christ or at least the clarity and honesty of a vigorous disbelief.

Jones remained hungry for conversion to an authentic faith. He needed a guide who could usher him into it. That guidance came two years later in the form of evangelist Robert J. Bateman, who came to Jones' church to preach in a series of meetings. Bateman was a converted alcoholic on fire for God. Jones told himself, "'I want what he has.' I would not be put off by catch phrases and slogans. I wanted the real thing or nothing."

For three days he sought it, going to the altar twice to pray. Before going to the meeting on the third night, Jones knelt by his bed "and prayed the sincerest prayer I had prayed so far in my life. My whole life was behind that simple prayer: 'O Jesus, save me tonight.' And He did! A ray of light pierced my darkness."

Jones went to the meeting that night and prayed publicly at the altar. This time he knew his conversion was real. "I had him—Jesus—and he had me. We had each other. I belonged. My estrangement, my sense of orphanage were gone. I was reconciled."[6] He wanted to "put my arms around the world and share this with everybody," and for the rest of his life that's what he did.

Another example of a person whose progress was delayed by the lack of a spiritual messenger is "Amazing Grace" author John Newton, whose story is told in the previous chapter. He ended up with a spiritual guide in the form of a fellow ship captain in London who clarified many issues of the Christian faith. Newton wrote, "For near a month, we spent every evening together, on board each other's ship alternately, and often prolonged our visits till towards daybreak. I was all ears; and what was better, he not only informed my understanding, but his discourse inflamed my heart."[7]

The strange thing is that Newton did not find this man until six years after he had become a Christian. Why hadn't someone emerged sooner to help this young Christian along? The near sinking of his ship was Newton's turning point toward Christ, and then for six years he was on his own to figure out what he could by reading the Bible multiple times and studying other good books.

For those of us who are already Christians, this underscores how important it is to be ready always to fulfill our role of spiritual messenger. Sometimes that may mean something very small—a word of encouragement, a quick prayer, a book we recommend, a question we answer. For other people our role may be much larger. We may teach a Sunday School class for months or years to a group of children or adults. We may spend weeks or months discussing our faith with a friend who's interested in spiritual issues. Like David in Linda Freeman's story, we may be there ready to pray with the person who is eager to move into a relationship with Jesus Christ.

These stories also highlight the fact that all of us need spiritual messengers. It's hard to find a single story of all the countless ones I have studied in which these guides did not play a crucial role. Look, for example, at the role Ananias played in Paul's "sudden" conversion. As the Lord spoke to Paul on the road to Damascus, he also appeared to Ananias in Damascus and prepared him to go to Paul and tell him about the important mission Paul was to carry out to take the gospel to the Gentiles.

Ananias went to Paul, delivered the message, and said, "Brother Saul, the Lord—Jesus, who appeared to you on the road as you were coming here—has sent me so that you may see again and be filled with the Holy Spirit" (Acts 9:17). Paul's sight was restored, he was baptized, and he spent several days with the disciples in Damascus. Ananias's role was crucial in Paul's story, and Paul needed the other disciples to help prepare him also.

If the apostle Paul needed spiritual messengers, then who doesn't? God chooses to use people to spread His gospel and work out His purposes among human beings. I'm eager to hear what He may have to tell me.

Go to www.beaconhillbooks.com/go/godinpursuit for a free downloadable Study Guide that includes questions for deeper personal reflection as well as activities for use in a small-group setting.

SIX

Tipping Point 3
When the Convicting Need for Spiritual Transformation Won't Let You Go

Jacquelyn was not a Christian, but she enjoyed going to the church close to her home. She liked the pastor's sermons, but sometimes they made her squirm. One Sunday in 1972, she "felt the pastor was looking straight into my soul," so without caring what anyone thought, she stood up during the sermon, left her seat, hurried up the center aisle, and left the church.

"What I felt, as I remember it," she said, "was that these people here were all good and holy people, but my heart was as black as black could be."

Nearly two hundred years earlier, sixteen-year-old Peter Cartwright felt something very similar. Fond of drinking, gambling, dancing, and horseracing on the American frontier in Kentucky, he rode his racehorse home from a wedding one night and sat by the fire, deep in thought. As he reflected on the way he had spent his day, he began to feel "guilty and condemned. I rose and walked the floor. My mother was in bed. It seemed to me, all of a sudden, my blood rushed to my head, my heart palpitated, in a few minutes I turned blind; an awful impression rested on my mind that death had come and I was unprepared to die. I fell on my knees and began to ask God to have mercy on me."

His mother got out of bed and started praying for her son. She urged him to turn to Christ for mercy. He did, but his ordeal was not over. The next morning he felt "wretched beyond expression." He did everything he could think of to relieve the guilt. He asked his father to sell his racehorse and asked his mother to burn his deck of cards. He tried to read the Bible and went off by himself throughout the day to pray. He fasted and prayed some more. "I was so distressed and miserable," he later wrote, "that I was incapable of any regular business."[1] His father was afraid his son might die and told him to stop working for a while.

Days passed with no relief. The local preacher came and prayed for him, and friends arrived to try to cheer him up. Cartwright's spiritual battle continued. His hope was briefly sparked when one day it "appeared to me that I heard a voice from heaven, saying, 'Peter, look at me.' A feeling of relief flashed over me as quick as an electric shock. It gave me hopeful feelings, and some encouragement to seek mercy, but still my load of guilt remained."

Three months went by before a series of revival meetings was held near Cartwright's home. He went forward at the end of one of the meetings and "earnestly prayed for mercy. In the midst of a solemn struggle of soul, an impression was made on my mind, as though a voice said to me, 'Thy sins are all forgiven thee.' Divine light flashed all round me, unspeakable joy sprung up in my soul. I rose to my feet, opened my eyes, and it really seemed as if I was in heaven; the trees, the leaves on them, and everything seemed, and I really thought were, praising God."[2]

The Meaning and Power of "Conviction"

The turning point toward faith in Jesus Christ for Jacquelyn Swinney in the early 1970s and Peter Cartwright was a force I don't hear much about anymore. When I was growing up, it was called "conviction" of sin. It's not a term I like to use. It sounds very old-fashioned. To me it conjures up images of manipulative, shouting, hellfire-and-damnation preachers trying to scare people into belief. It puts the focus on "guilt" and "sin," when I would much rather emphasize Jesus' loving, inviting, presence that draws us to Him.

But at the heart of Christianity is the idea that all have sinned and need God's forgiveness and salvation. Conviction is a process by which we may come to sense that need deep within. Without it, salvation for some people would never move beyond an abstract, distant concept, and they would never feel the need to turn to God.

In earlier chapters I talked about the limitations of language to get at the essence of certain aspects of spiritual experience, and conviction is one of the places where for me the words don't quite describe what actually happens.

Let's take the concept of sin and salvation. C. S. Lewis, one of the clearest Christian writers ever, wrote in *Mere Christianity*, "We are told that Christ was killed for us, that His death washed out our sins, and that by dying He disabled death itself. That is the formula. That is Christianity. That is what has to be believed." On the next page he describes repentance: "Laying down your arms, surrendering, saying you are sorry, realizing that you have been on the wrong track and getting ready to start life over again from the ground floor—that is the only way out of our 'hole.' This process of surrender—this movement full speed astern—is what Christians call repentance."[3]

That is a great short explanation, one of the best I've seen. When I was in college, I read Lewis's book and was stunned by how well he explained the faith I had been part of since I was eight years old.

And yet for me, as for many readers, it's easy to keep those ideas at a distance. They are concepts. Intellectually, I like how he explains them, but they don't hit me at the deep level of experience. Other writers put even more distance between me and the reality of sin and repentance. Here's an excerpt from a well-written definition of salvation from a theological dictionary: "Salvation is therefore, first, acquittal, despite just condemnation, on the ground of Christ's expiation of sin (Romans 3:21-22), and, second, deliverance by the invasive power of the Spirit of holiness, the Spirit of the Risen Christ. The faith which accepts and assents to Christ's death on our behalf also unites us to him so closely that with him we die to sin and rise to new life (Romans 6:1-12)."[4]

I believe all of that, and I'm grateful for the theologian who wrote about it with such precision. These writers help me understand sin, but conviction is what makes me *know*—what makes me sense at a deep, urgent level—that I am filled with sin and that only Jesus Christ can cleanse me of it. Conviction is a gift that God gives me that opens my eyes to the truth of what I really am. I believe it is not His way of *persuading* me that I am sin-filled so much as it is His way of simply turning the spotlight on that sin and pointing my eyes toward it so that I can see it.

That glimpse into the dark truth about oneself can be so disturbing that, in Jacquelyn's case, it sent her fleeing the sanctuary. It can be so painful that it causes the deep agony and guilt that Peter Cartwright suffered. It's also possible to ignore the conviction, or explain it away, or to be so resistant to the Holy Spirit that we don't let it penetrate us in the first place.

I experienced conviction before I had a name for it when I became a Christian at the end of a week of Vacation Bible School. Conviction was not the first or even main force that drew me to God. What attracted me first was the love of the church people. I loved the teachers and stories and music. I sensed the love and power of the Holy Spirit in this place and wanted to keep coming back.

I felt God's presence drawing me to Him, but at the moment of decision, when the pastor gave the invitation for those who want to give their lives to Jesus to come down and pray, I also sensed the unmistakable dread that I *needed* forgiveness. Like Jacquelyn, I felt that the pastor was peering into my very soul when he preached from Romans 3:23, that I, like everyone else, had "sinned and fall[en] short of the glory of God." I didn't need elaborate explanations or definitions of sin and forgiveness and salvation (I would seek such explanations later). I understood sin perfectly well. It's not as hard for an eight-year-old boy to fathom as some might think.

I had enough conviction within me to know that I was a sinner, and I had enough of a tug from the Holy Spirit that I knew Jesus Christ was the only way out of this dilemma. I struggled for a short time to try to deny and explain away my predicament, but not as much as I would struggle against God later during times of spiritual crisis. I walked to the altar that day with the complexity of feelings that I imagine the prodigal son would have had as he walked back to his father. Part of me didn't want to go, but I knew I needed Jesus. I felt the joy of His love and forgiveness wash over me. I was a Christian.

Not Everyone Experiences Conviction in the Same Way

Repentance and forgiveness are essential elements of Christian conversion, but not everyone reaches that by way of the kind of conviction of sin I have described. Conversion requires an insight into one's sinful nature and a turning toward Christ, forgiveness, and salvation, but wrestling with guilt is not necessarily what triggers that insight or turning.

For example, Richard V. Peace argues that Paul's turn to Christ did not arise from a guilty conscience but rather from his insight that he had been wrong about who Jesus was. There was no agonizing with guilt over his pre-Christian actions, at least not any that's revealed in Scripture. Paul did what he thought was right up to the moment he met Jesus on the road to Damascus, and then once he realized the truth, he made the turn to become a follower of Christ. Peace mentions others in the Bible whose turn to Christ was not triggered by a guilty conscience:

The Ethiopian is drawn to Jesus out of his interest in prophecy (Acts 8:31-35). It is fear that drives the Philippian jailer to conversion (Acts 16:27-30). Cornelius is a pious Gentile upon whom (along with his whole household) the Holy Spirit descends, leading to their conversion (Acts 10). It is the experience of the power of God that brings about this turning to God. Prior to his conversion Cornelius is described as "a devout man who feared God with all his household; he gave alms generously to the people and prayed constantly to God" (Acts 10:2). The point is that to define conversion as a response to a guilty conscience is to limit the concept far too severely and, in fact, to define conversion in a way that the Bible does not.[5]

"I Feared the Ground Would Cleave Asunder . . . and Become My Grave"

Even for those for whom conviction of sin is an important turning point toward Christ, the intensity of that struggle varies widely. It's more common in conversion stories from earlier centuries, when the problem of sin was more emphasized. In those days the awareness of sin for some people was so severe that it could be almost paralyzing. David Brainerd, who converted to Christianity in New England in 1739 and later became a missionary to the Indians, wrote this in his diary:

> One night I remember in particular, when I was walking solitarily abroad, I had opened to me such a view of my sin that I feared the ground would cleave asunder under my feet and become my grave; and would send my soul quick into hell, before I could get home. Though I was forced to go to bed, lest my distress should be discovered by others, which I much feared; yet I scarcely durst sleep at all, for I thought it would be great wonder if I should be out of hell in the morning.[6]

I could cite many examples much like that from the Puritan era and earlier. For many of us today, the language comes across as jarring and extreme, all that wallowing in guilt and fear. But the converts don't stay there. That's not where they live their Christian lives. Instead, like those converts described earlier whose turning point was suffering, this conviction of sin serves to *awaken* the person to a central Christian belief: there's nothing inherent about them that is so good, and they can do nothing through their own good living, to earn their salvation. They are entirely dependent on the mercy and forgiveness of Jesus Christ. Paul and others came to the same conclusion, but by different means. Once conviction of sin has awakened people to their need for Christ, they can then turn to Him to find overwhelming love and forgiveness.

Brainerd, for example, was more bothered by the *easing* of the sense of conviction than he was about the distress of the conviction itself. The reason is that he could sense that God was using the conviction to draw him to salvation, and he feared drifting away from that back to a sense of complacency.

> When at any time I took a view of my convictions, and thought the degree of them to be considerable, I was wont to trust in them, but this confidence, and the hopes of soon making some notable advances towards deliverance, would ease my mind, and I soon became more senseless and remiss. Again, when I discerned my convictions to grow languid, and thought them about to leave me; this immediately alarmed and distressed me.[7]

When Brainerd's conversion finally came, he described it in terms just as dramatic as the painful sense of conviction that led up to it. This was an age in which people took spiritual matters seriously. They read books of sermons for entertainment. Questions of one's relationship to God touched the core of their emotions. Brainerd was a man who wanted to reach God by trying so hard to be good that the Lord would have no choice but to grant him salvation. The conviction wiped away this false self-confidence and helped him realize deep down that only Christ could save him. When he reached the low point of his confidence in his own ability to achieve salvation, his religious affections dried up and he found himself in a "mournful melancholy state."

That's when Jesus arrived. As Brainerd walked in a grove, trying unsuccessfully to pray, *"unspeakable glory* seemed to open to
the view and apprehension of my soul." God's presence was so overwhelming that he could do nothing but stand in awe. "My soul *re-
joiced with joy unspeakable,* to see such a God, such a glorious divine
Being; and I was inwardly pleased and satisfied, that he should be
God over all for ever and ever." At first, Brainerd was so "swallowed
up" by God's presence that he gave no thought to his own salvation
and came close to even forgetting "that there was such a creature as
myself." He stood there in that state of joy until nearly dark.

> At this time, the *way of salvation* opened to me with such
> infinite wisdom, suitableness, and excellency, that I wondered
> I should ever think of any other way of salvation; was amazed
> that I had not dropped my own contrivances, and complied
> with this lovely, blessed, and excellent way before.[8]

"My Self-Centered Past Was Washing Over Me in Waves"

Conviction and conversion are often expressed in less emotional
language in our day, but the transformation they bring can be just
as life-changing. One more recent convert who deeply felt the sting
of conviction was Charles Colson, one of United States President
Richard Nixon's top aides at the center of the Watergate scandal.
Colson served time in prison for his role in that scandal and later
started the Prison Fellowship ministry and wrote many books.

David Brainerd grew up in a world steeped in Christian theology, scripture, and the church, but Colson lived in a world in which
success in politics was the center of existence. In the dark days of
Watergate, when Colson's friend Tom Phillips told him about his
relationship with Jesus Christ, Colson said he "had not even been
aware that finding a personal relationship with God was possible."[9]

Colson was skeptical of Christianity and would have dismissed
the whole thing as "pure Pollyanna" except that he respected his
friend, who was a powerful and successful businessman in addition

to being a Christian. The conviction set in when Tom read Colson a portion of C. S. Lewis's *Mere Christianity*. It was a section on the sin of pride, which leads to every other vice. It says that pride "has been the chief cause of misery in every nation and every family since the world began. . . . [It] is a spiritual cancer: it eats up the very possibility of love, or contentment, or even common sense."

As he listened to those words, Nixon's hatchet man said he suddenly "felt naked and unclean, my bravado defenses gone. I was exposed, unprotected, for Lewis's words were describing me." As he contemplated Lewis's words, "my self-centered past was washing over me in waves. It was painful. Agony." He tried to find excuses for himself to explain away his guilt, but he couldn't. The sin of pride had defined—and now threatened to destroy—his life and career, and for the first time he felt the full force of his guilt.

Colson did not accept Tom's invitation to repent and turn to Jesus that night, but it was the turning point in his conversion, which came later. As he left Tom's house and tried to drive home, he was so overcome with emotion that he had to pull the car to the side of the road. He sobbed, and as he did, he "began to experience a wonderful feeling of being released. Then came the strange sensation that water was not only running down my cheeks, but surging through my body as well, cleansing and cooling as it went. They weren't tears of sadness and remorse, nor of joy—but somehow, tears of relief." Then he prayed his first real prayer: "God, I don't know how to find you, but I'm going to try! I'm not much the way I am now, but somehow I want to give myself to you."[10] Not knowing what else to pray, he repeated the words *Take me.*

Colson didn't yet know who Jesus Christ really was and wanted to find out more about Him before he committed his life to Him, but in a very powerful sense, God had already taken hold of Colson. His conversion came after further soul-searching, prayer, and grappling with the message of the gospel as Lewis presents it in *Mere Christianity*. Finally, as Colson "sat alone staring at the sea I love,

210588

88

words I had not been certain I could understand or say fell naturally from my lips: 'Lord Jesus, I believe you. I accept you. Please come into my life. I commit it to you.'"[11]

"You Can Come to Him Just as You Are"

Billy Graham has spoken in person to more people than anyone else in history—more than 210 million. Hundreds of thousands of people have converted to Christianity at his crusades throughout the world.[12] His presentation of the gospel is simple and direct. Much of his message relies on the power of the Holy Spirit to persuade—or "convict"—people of the need for salvation, and then he gives them the opportunity to come forward and turn to God based on that need. His invitation has remained very similar over the years, and it's this:

> I'm going to ask you to get out of your seat and come and stand quietly and reverently as an indication that you're receiving Christ, that you want a new heart and a new life from this moment on, that you're going to allow Him to change the direction of your life. The Holy Spirit has been speaking. He's been preparing your heart. Now you come and receive Christ. If you're with friends or relatives, they'll wait on you. I'm not going to keep you long. But I'm asking you to come and stand here and say by coming, "I give my life to Christ. I want a new life. I want a new heart. I want forgiveness of my past. I want Christ in my life and in my heart."[13]

For all its old-fashioned connotations of guilt and condemnation, conviction of sin is actually a tool of the Holy Spirit that opens people's eyes to the truth about themselves and lights the path to Jesus as their only hope.

Go to www.beaconhillbooks.com/go/godinpursuit for a free downloadable Study Guide that includes questions for deeper personal reflection as well as activities for use in a small-group setting.

SEVEN

Tipping Point 4
When the Word Speaks with
Undeniable Clarity and Power

Here's what surprises me about the role the Bible plays in the conversions of many people to Christianity. To me the Bible seems so long and complex and strangely organized that it's hard to imagine that someone who's never encountered it before could pick it up on his or her own and make sense of it. What would prevent the person from getting bogged down in the long lists of rules in Deuteronomy or the interminable genealogies of 1 Chronicles or the difficult prophecies of Isaiah? How could this book strike so deeply that an unbeliever could not only understand it but also follow it as a guide to his or her faith in Christ? That sounds like an unlikely path to conversion for people previously unfamiliar with Scripture, but I've encountered one conversion story after another in which the Bible plays such a role.

One of the most unlikely converts to Christianity that I ran across was Mary Kay Beard. While still in her twenties, she stumbled into a life of crime that eventually landed her on the FBI's Ten Most Wanted list. Her range of crimes was amazing—she shoplifted books from bookstores and stole cash from the Mafia, leading them to put a contract out on her life.

As recounted in Jodi Werhanowicz's book *Rogue Angel*, Mary Kay robbed banks and cracked safes. While married to a crooked gambler, she sewed magnets into the pockets of her dress to make the loaded dice fall the right way. When her husband later was thrown in jail, she smuggled in razor blades and a hacksaw taped to her body and helped him escape.

Her crimes continued, but eventually, at age twenty-eight, she was sentenced to twenty-one years in prison for armed robbery and grand larceny.[1] She felt as if her life was over.

She didn't know that the best part was just beginning.

While in solitary confinement, Mary Kay began attending a church service on Sunday mornings in order to escape the boredom of her cell. She was familiar with Christianity but felt bitter toward it. Her mother had been a Christian, but her father had been mean and abusive and had made her childhood miserable. Now she wanted only to kill some time. "She determined to be just difficult enough to irritate these religious folks but not enough to be banned from going to church altogether," wrote Werhanowicz. "She had to get out of that miserable cell, no matter what."[2] A weekly Bible study on Tuesday afternoons also offered a diversion from her jail cell, so Mary Kay started attending that too.

One or Two Verses of Scripture Can Make All the Difference

Careful study of the entire Bible is an important part of the spiritual journey of many who turn to Christ, but the turning point to salvation is often only one or two verses. That pattern is repeated in countless conversion stories.

Sometimes the verses are ones people learned years ago but that now come back to their minds with a power and meaning they never had for them before. These encounters with scripture are good examples of *kairos*, or "loaded time," when people seem most open to the intervention of the Holy Spirit in their lives. The words of the verses themselves, which the person may have read dozens of times before, now come to life as if filled with the presence of the Holy Spirit.

After Mary Kay Beard started attending the prison church services and Bible study, she went back to her cell one day and picked up her own Bible. It was a Gideon-placed Bible that been issued to her and that she had stuffed under her pillow when she moved into her cell. She looked at it only out of desperation. She felt increasing remorse for what she had done with her life, but what could she do about it? Flipping through the pages of the Bible, she landed on Ezekiel 36:26-27: "A new heart also will I give you, and a new spirit will I put within you: and I will take away the stony heart out of your flesh . . . and I will put my spirit within you, and cause you to walk in my statutes, and ye shall keep my judgments, and do them" (KJV).

This scripture was the turning point for Mary Kay Beard. It didn't turn her around in some magical or sentimental way. She studied it. In fact, remembering a grammar technique she had learned in third grade, she diagrammed the sentence in her mind. She realized that God was the one doing the action in those sentences. It was not up to her to make herself good enough to deserve His salvation. "She did not have to do anything except show up, present herself, say yes, and receive. God would empower her to do what He wanted her to do." She prayed, "Father, if you mean that verse for me, if you will give me a new heart and make me the kind of person you want me to be, I'll give my life to you. Wherever you want me to go, whatever you want me to do, that's what I will do."[3]

As she rose from her knees and sat down on her bunk, Mary Kay felt a strange sensation that she remembered from her mother, who had been a Christian. It was "the peace that passes understanding." Mary Kay felt deep gratitude and knew that she now belonged to Christ.

When One Passage of Scripture Rises to the Surface

Flipping through the Bible and landing on a verse sounds like a random and terrible way to do Bible study, and Mary Kay went far beyond that later, reading and studying the entire Bible multiple times. But so many conversion stories include scripture that emerges in seemingly random ways that I have to believe this is one of the ways the Holy Spirit uses to reach people.

The emergence of key scripture is never a substitute for the more deliberate and in-depth study of the Bible that should take place throughout the Christian life, but God seems to have ways of highlighting particular verses at crucial moments. In rock star Brian Welch's story discussed earlier, for instance, the verses from Matthew 11 about taking on Christ's yoke and finding rest for your soul popped up so often in his life that when it appeared on the screen at church one day, he thought, mistakenly, that someone was deliberately toying with him by placing it there.

One of the most famous conversions in Christian history includes just such a bizarre element of one life-changing verse of Scripture being brought to the forefront in an amazing way. Augustine, the great theologian and one of the Early Church fathers, who lived in the years 354 to 430 in North Africa, tells his story in his *Confessions*.

Augustine was in agony of spirit and "angry at myself with a turbulent indignation because I had not entered thy will and covenant, O my God, while all my bones cried out to me to enter, extolling to the skies." He sat in the garden of his house with a friend named Alypius, but as Augustine descended further into misery, he went off a little farther by himself so that he could fully give way to his tears. He cried and called out to God, "How long, how long? Tomorrow and tomorrow? Why not now? Why not this very hour make an end to my uncleanness?"

God answered his prayer in an unexpected way. As he prayed and wept, next door he heard the voice of a child repeatedly chanting, "Pick it up; read it; pick it up; read it." He couldn't think of any game that would cause a child to chant such words, so it occurred to him that perhaps it was a divine message to him. He went back to the book of Scripture he had left by where Alypius was sitting,

> snatched it up, opened it, and in silence read the paragraph on which my eyes first fell: "Not in rioting and drunkenness, not in chambering and wantonness, not in strife and envying, put on the Lord Jesus Christ, and make no provision for the flesh to fulfill the lusts thereof." I wanted to read no further, nor did I need to. For instantly, as the sentence ended, there was infused in my heart something like the light of full certainty and all the gloom of doubt vanished away.

Augustine told his friend what had happened, and Alypius wanted to see the scripture for himself. Once he saw it, he read a little further and found Romans 14:1, which says to receive those who are weak in the faith. Alypius was going through his own spiritual crisis and applied the words to himself. He joined Augustine "in full commitment without any restless hesitation."[4]

In the Scripture-soaked 1700s and 1800s in America and England, the examples of people for whom short passages of Scripture were the turning point to faith in Jesus Christ are abundant. Jonathan Edwards, one of the most important preachers and theologians of The Great Awakening era in the United States in the eighteenth century, reached a turning point on his path toward conversion when he read these words from 1 Timothy 1:17—"Now unto the King eternal, immortal, invisible, the only wise God, be honour and glory for ever and ever. Amen" (KJV).

As he read this verse, there came into his soul "a sense of the glory of the Divine Being; a new sense, quite different from any thing I ever experienced before." The words made him think

> how excellent a Being that was, and how happy I should be, if I might enjoy that God, and be rapt up to him in heaven, and be as it were swallowed up in him for ever! I kept saying, and as it were singing, over these words of scripture to myself; and

went to pray to God that I might enjoy him, and prayed in a manner quite different from what I used to do; with a new sort of affection.[5]

In many of these cases in which one portion of Scripture emerges with new significance for the person, the words captivate him or her on many levels at once—intellectually, spiritually, and emotionally. For Charles G. Finney, who would become an important revivalist preacher of the nineteenth century, the biblical passage that entered his mind at the crucial moment was one that he wasn't even consciously aware that he knew. As he struggled in prayer, seeking forgiveness for the sin that weighed heavily on him, "this passage of Scripture seemed to drop into my mind with a flood of light: 'Then shall ye go and pray unto me, and I will hearken unto you. Then shall ye seek me and find me, when ye shall search for me with all your heart'" (Jeremiah 29:12, KJV).

Finney said he somehow "knew that that was a passage of Scripture, though I do not think I had ever read it. I knew that it was God's word, and God's voice, as it were, that spoke to me." As he continued in prayer, Finney says the Holy Spirit continued to bring passages of Scripture to his mind. God was using the Bible to bring him to salvation even though he didn't actually have a Bible there with him. Finney says he had believed the Bible before, but only intellectually.

Now, the words "did not seem so much to fall into my intellect as into my heart, to be put within the grasp of the voluntary powers of my mind; and I seized hold of them, appropriated them, and fastened upon them with the grasp of a drowning man."[6] Finney continued his prayer and spiritual struggle throughout the rest of that day and into the night until his conversion was complete.

When One Verse Sparks a Deeper Study of Scripture

Sunshine Harris was an alcoholic living in a filthy room on skid row in Chicago in 1899. One night he came home drunk, kicked opened his door, and fell onto his bed. For some reason he also opened a New Testament, and when he had opened it and had managed to focus his eyes well enough to read from it, he read aloud, "Thou fool, this night thy soul shall be required of thee."

Harris did not believe in God, so as the book fell to the floor, he said, "Never heard such rot in my life. Makes me mad." It made him so angry, in fact, that he stomped around the room, kicking empty bottles and grinding cigarette butts into the floor. Then he lay back down, exhausted. He tried to remember the verse that had sparked his anger. "Thou fool . . . this night . . ." The verse would not come back to him. Even though he thought it was "bunk," he still had to know what it said.

He decided he would have to start from the beginning of the book until he found it. Even though it might take him all week, he would keep at it until he found that verse. He opened to Matthew 1 and started with the genealogy of Jesus Christ. He read through chapter after chapter of Jesus' life and teachings, until finally he found the verse he was looking for. By then, however, that verse wasn't his only concern. He had started to actually believe what he was reading. He had reached the tipping point into faith.

That night Harris visited the Pacific Garden Mission, where he was a familiar—and skeptical and cantankerous—figure, and came forward at the end of the worship service to turn his life over to Christ.[7]

How God Did It: Behind the Scenes of a Loaded Moment with Scripture

Scripture alone is sometimes enough to lead someone to Christ, but in other cases the person also needs a "spiritual messenger," like those discussed in an earlier chapter, to help dig out the meaning of the words. One of the most powerful examples of this is a conversion story in the Bible itself. In Acts 8 an Ethiopian royal court official has traveled a tremendous distance to worship in Jerusalem, and on his long chariot ride back to Ethiopia, he reads out loud from the Book of Isaiah. He doesn't understand what he's reading.

In what to outsiders would have looked like a coincidence but is actually a "loaded moment" prepared by God, Philip runs up to this chariot on a desert road just as the Ethiopian reads a portion that says, "He was led like a sheep to the slaughter, and as a lamb before the shearer is silent, so he did not open his mouth. In his humiliation he was deprived of justice. Who can speak of his descendants?" (Acts 8:32-33). Philip asks him if he understands what he is reading, and the man asks, "How can I . . . unless someone explains it to me?" (Acts 8:31). The Ethiopian asks Philip whether Isaiah is referring to himself in the passage or someone else. Philip starts with that scripture and tells him all about Jesus.

As they travel down the road and come to some water, the Ethiopian says, "Look, here is water. Why shouldn't I be baptized?" (Acts 8:36). Philip takes him down to the water and baptizes him, and then the man goes on his way rejoicing.

Although many conversion stories contain "loaded moments" like this, we rarely get a glimpse of how God sets them up. But this story also goes behind the scenes to show how God puts all the elements in place so that the seeker's questions can be answered and he can make a decision about whether he'll follow Christ. First, an angel of the Lord directs Philip to go to the desert road between Jerusalem and Gaza. Philip goes, not knowing why he's going or what he's supposed to do when he gets there. Philip meets the Ethiopian on the way, and the Holy Spirit directs him to stay near his chariot. That's when the loaded moment of opportunity comes as the man begins reading out loud from Isaiah. Afterwards, once Philip baptizes the man, "the Spirit of the Lord suddenly took Philip away," and the Ethiopian never sees him again (Acts 8:39).

Few conversion stories contain so many supernatural aspects, and we can't expect the Holy Spirit to intervene in such an observable way very often, but this story shows how active the Spirit is in creating opportunities for people to make a decision about following Christ. It also shows what many other conversion stories have illustrated—that scripture is often a key element in opening the person's understanding of God.

After Conversion, Scripture Continues to Blaze

The Bible remained a central element of the spiritual lives of all of these people after conversion. In the two years following her turn to Christ, Mary Kay Beard read the Bible straight through eight times. Augustine, Jonathan Edwards, and Charles Finney became important church leaders and writers who studied the Bible carefully and knew it intimately. The Holy Spirit speaks through that long-term, daily reading and meditation on the Bible just as powerfully as He does in the more dramatic moments when one verse blazes forth with new meaning.

Mary Kay Beard's love of the Bible was so strong that she started her own Bible study in the prison. Even though she was now a Christian, her circumstances were still bleak. She was transferred to a state prison in Alabama to serve out her sentence, and that's where she started her Bible class for fellow prisoners. As far as she knew, that might have been her only ministry opportunity for the next twenty years, but God continued to intervene in her life. The Gideons International found out about her conversion and invited her to speak at one of their conventions. She was given permission to take a trip outside the prison to do this, and many other speaking engagements followed.

A few years after Mary Kay got out of prison on parole in 1978, she started the ministry for which she is best known, the Angel Tree program, which is part of Chuck Colson's Prison Fellowship. The idea was to provide a way for the children of prisoners to receive Christmas gifts. Shoppers could choose an angel from a tree, and on it was written the name of a child and a suggested gift. The shopper could buy the gift and give it to the volunteers to deliver to the child.

According to Colson, the Angel Tree ministry "is now reaching well over half a million children every year, sending over 10,000 children to Christian camp, and enabling nearly 1,000 children to be mentored by loving adults."[8] It operates in all fifty states in the United States and in fifty other countries.

It's easy for many Christians to let the Bible become a dormant document. They believe in it, they revere it, they don't mind hearing it read in church, but they cease to be awake to the fact that it's a living, breathing set of words through which God speaks and works. It accomplishes nothing in us if it's simply a prop we carry with us to church, but as we let it seep deeply into us, it can light our way to salvation and to a more joyful relationship with God.

Go to www.beaconhillbooks.com/go/godinpursuit for a free downloadable Study Guide that includes questions for deeper personal reflection as well as activities for use in a small-group setting.

EIGHT

Tipping Point 5
When a Long Intellectual and Spiritual Persuasion Pushes You Toward Christ

When Paul encountered Jesus Christ as he headed toward Damascus to round up Christians in order to imprison them, he was not granted several weeks or months to sit down and marshal a list of arguments for and against becoming a Christian. He answered the call right away and obeyed Christ.

When Joe Eszterhas sat suffering, near death, on a sidewalk in Ohio, he turned to God immediately to cry out for rescue.

When the call of Jesus Christ interrupted Jim Vaus's trip to carry out a job for a mobster, he gave his life to Jesus that night and abandoned his criminal career.

For these converts and many others discussed so far, the tipping point toward faith involves a life-changing encounter with the Holy Spirit, followed by conversion, followed by years of working out the intellectual and spiritual questions this new faith raises.

For others, the turn toward Christianity is a much slower and more deliberate process that takes years and sometimes decades. Some reach the tipping point so gradually that they don't fully recognize it when it comes. A woman named Doane Wylie told me,

My coming to faith can probably be likened to taking a few steps across a room. When I started, I was an unbeliever, and when I stopped, I was a believer. Somewhere in that left-foot-right-foot-repeat-as-necessary (my son's description of walking) I said to myself, "I believe that"—"that" being the need to acknowledge my need for the forgiveness of my sin. I don't think the true salvation message ever really sunk in with me until that point, even though I may have heard it many times. But I guess the Holy Spirit just tapped a little harder on my shoulder that time.

These converts who turn to Christ gradually, including people like Francis Collins, C. S. Lewis, and Malcolm Muggeridge, often start their move toward Christianity from a stance of atheism or agnosticism. Many questions have to be answered, and many intellectual and spiritual barriers must be knocked down before they'll consider becoming Christians. In many of these cases, embracing Christianity would put them at odds with many of their peers professionally and would require them to contradict many of their own previous arguments against the faith.

Because becoming a Christian would be so disruptive, they've often built up elaborate intellectual defenses against it. Once those walls finally crumble, however, and these skeptics become believers, they're already so familiar with the arguments against Christianity that they often turn into some of the most articulate advocates of the faith.

I Don't Believe in God

The atheism in the early lives of some of these converts seems so entrenched that it looks impregnable. One vivid example is Francis Collins, best known for leading a team of scientists who achieved one of the greatest scientific breakthroughs of the twentieth century, the human genome project.

The human genome, the hereditary code of life, comprises all the DNA of our species. The text of this code is so complex that it's 3 billion letters long. The human genome project brought Collins and his colleagues worldwide renown. The president of the United States honored Collins and his team at the White House, and celebrations took place worldwide to extol this scientific breakthrough.

An issue a scientist of Collins' caliber must confront is *how compatible are science and Christianity?* Is it possible to hold sophisticated, scientifically credible views on scientific issues such as the origin of life and also believe that Jesus Christ is the Son of God, who brings salvation and eternal life?

Collins was first an agnostic and later an atheist. He grew up in a family in which education was valued and in which faith was not important. He studied chemistry in college and eventually entered a Ph.D. in physical chemistry at Yale University. Influenced by other scientists who did not believe in God, Collins came to the "conclusion that no thinking scientist could seriously entertain the possibility of God without committing some sort of intellectual suicide."

Once he had settled on that conclusion, he thought he was finished with questions about God and faith. "I felt quite comfortable challenging the spiritual beliefs of anyone who mentioned them in my presence," he said, "and discounted such perspectives as sentimentality and outmoded superstition."[1]

C. S. Lewis, now one of the most popular Christian writers in the world, was as adamant as Collins in dismissing the reality and relevance of God and Christianity. Although he was raised in a stale church tradition and had thought of himself as a Christian as a young boy, at age thirteen he "ceased to be a Christian." In *Surprised by Joy* he traces the various reasons for this movement into disbelief, such as an interest in the occult, a flawed concept of prayer, and a sense that Christianity was just one of a thousand religions out there and not much more likely to be true than any of the others.

Lewis threw off the Christian religion "with no sense of loss but with the greatest relief." He wrote that "From the tyrannous noon of revelation I passed into the cool evening of Higher Thought, where there was nothing to be obeyed, and nothing to be believed except what was either comforting or exciting."[2]

Malcolm Muggeridge, who became famous as a foreign correspondent, biographer of Mother Teresa, and television personality, was an outspoken agnostic for much of his career and did not come to Christ until he was in his eighties. In his spiritual memoir, *Conversion*, Muggeridge shows God lurking at the fringes of his life at many stages from boyhood on. Muggeridge often came close to complete commitment to Christ before pulling back at the last minute. It was hard for him to fully embrace belief, but he had just as much trouble fully embracing disbelief. The war within him included many battles and took decades to play out.

The Walls of Disbelief Begin to Crumble

No single encounter proved decisive as Collins, Lewis, and Muggeridge inched their way toward Christianity. Instead, these three converts would sense God's slow, steady pursuit of them over time. Their movement to faith would involve not one turning point but many, as various books, people, ideas, and experiences emerged to lead them down winding and broken paths to Jesus Christ.

Near the end of his Ph.D. program, Francis Collins applied to medical school and became a doctor. One of his turning points toward Christianity was a conversation he had with one of his severely ill patients. Collins had often been impressed by the strong sense of reassurance the faith of some of his patients gave them. One day one of them shared her strong Christian beliefs with him and then asked him what he believed. He could do nothing but stammer out the words "I'm really not sure."

Although his atheism was a settled belief, this encounter made him realize that he had never taken the time to weigh the evidence for and against Christianity. Her question haunted him. He thought,

> Did I not consider myself a scientist? Does a scientist draw conclusions without considering the data? Could there be a more important question in all of human existence than "Is there a God?" And yet there I found myself, with a combination of willful blindness and something that could only be properly described as arrogance, having avoided any serious consideration that God might be a real possibility.[3]

His search for answers began. Atheism had allowed Collins not to have to think much about issues of faith, and investigating God was a "thoroughly terrifying experience" that pushed him into realms of thought he would have preferred to leave alone. But the question of God's existence and what it might mean to him personally was now too burning to ignore. He approached his investigation the way he would any question in his own field of science—he studied the various world religions. In the midst of this process, someone recommended a book written a generation earlier by another intellectually gifted man who had once been an atheist, C. S. Lewis. The book was *Mere Christianity*, and Lewis became Collins' spiritual guide as he found his way to Christ.

Collins was amazed at the way Lewis's book anticipated and dealt with one after another of Collins' own objections to Christianity. One of Lewis's arguments that Collins found most powerful was his treatment of the idea of the moral law. A sense of right and wrong seems to be built into people, even though they disagree on the details of which behaviors fit which category. People appeal to a sense of fairness and justice, but where does that sense come from? It crosses cultures and time periods. Is the moral law merely a consequence of evolutionary pressures? How can altruism be explained by evolution? Collins pondered these issues, which he deals with in greater detail in his book *The Language of God*. He came to believe that the moral law could not be explained away as a cultural artifact or evolutionary byproduct.

Furthermore, if God existed, would science be able to locate Him in the creation itself, or would He stand outside it as Creator? He encountered this argument from Lewis:

> If there was a controlling power outside the universe, it could not show itself to us as one of the facts inside the universe—no more than the architect of a house could actually be a wall or staircase or fireplace in that house. The only way in which we could expect it to show itself would be inside ourselves as an influence or a command trying to get us to behave in a certain way. And that is just what we do find inside ourselves. Surely this ought to arouse our suspicions?

Collins said that when he read this, he was

> stunned by its logic. Here, hiding in my own heart as familiar as anything in daily experience, but now emerging for the first time as a clarifying principle, this Moral Law shone its bright white light into the recesses of my childish atheism, and demanded a serious consideration of its own origin. Was this God looking back at me?

Up to this time, science had been Collins's guiding light, and he would still put it to life-changing use and become one of the most acclaimed scientists in the world. However, he realized that, useful as it was, science simply did not have the capacity to answer every kind of question. He wrote, "It also became clear to me that science, despite its unquestioned powers in unraveling the mysteries of the natural world, would get me no further in resolving the question of God. If God exists, then He must be outside the natural world, and therefore the tools of science are not the right ones to learn about Him."

The evidence would have to come from elsewhere, and ultimately he would have to rely on "faith, not proof."[4]

Like his spiritual mentor, Lewis, before him, Collins converted to theism first and then had to probe even deeper to determine whether he believed that Jesus Christ and the Christian faith were the true manifestations of the God he now believed existed. Collins' belief in the moral law indicated that God must be a holy and righteous God who cared about people, or else there would be no need for moral law. Collins also became increasingly aware of how far he fell short of consistently living up to a high standard of righteousness.

No matter how hard he tried, he could not extinguish the pride, apathy, and anger that kept surfacing in his attitudes and actions. "I had never really thought of applying the word 'sinner' to myself before," he wrote, "but now it was painfully obvious that this old-fashioned word, one from which I had previously recoiled because it seemed coarse and judgmental, fit quite accurately."

Could Jesus Christ be the bridge between his sinful self and a holy God? Did the death and resurrection of Christ provide atonement for sin, and did it make the way for Collins to experience the death of pride and sinfulness that blocked him from being spiritually reborn as a new creation? He carefully examined the theology of Christianity, but that was not enough. What about the historical accuracy of Jesus? "The scientist in me refused to go any further along this path toward Christian belief, no matter how appealing, if the biblical writings about Christ turned out to be a myth, or worse yet, a hoax." His research into history satisfied him about the historical accuracy of Jesus' existence.

A year had passed since Collins's conversion to theism, and all his probing of Christianity led him toward the belief that it was true. It was time to make a decision. He hesitated. He still had doubts. He knew a leap of faith would be necessary, and he took it on a beautiful fall day on a hiking trip in the Cascade Mountains. The "majesty and beauty of God's creation overwhelmed my resistance. As I rounded a corner and saw a beautiful and unexpected frozen waterfall, hundreds of feet high, I knew the search was over. The next morning, I knelt in the dewy grass as the sun rose and surrendered to Jesus Christ."[5]

Francis Collins was now a Christian, but he was not at the end of his questioning. In his book he confronts other intellectual barriers that he and others have had to overcome as they contemplate becoming Christians, such as the problem of suffering, the notion that belief in God might simply be wishful thinking, the problem of the atrocities that have been committed in the name of religion, and scientific issues of evolution and the origin of the universe.

He continues to be a committed Christian and a committed scientist. He asks,

> In this modern era of cosmology, evolution, and the human genome, is there still the possibility of a richly satisfying harmony between the scientific and spiritual worldviews? I answer with a resounding yes! In my view, there is no conflict in being a rigorous scientist and a person who believes in a God who takes a personal interest in each one of us.[6]

"The Most Dejected and Reluctant Convert in All England"

C. S. Lewis, through his books, was an ideal spiritual mentor for Francis Collins, because even though these two men worked in different intellectual realms—Collins in science and Lewis in literature and philosophy—both of them had inched their way from atheism to Christianity in a deliberate, thoughtful, and intellectually rigorous way. Both were open to unexpected, jarring insights. Both were willing to go where the truth led them no matter how uncomfortable that place might be.

The multiplicity of influences that led Lewis to faith in Jesus Christ are too numerous to present in detail here, but a few points along his path are worth looking at. Lewis, like other converts we've seen, felt pursued by God. He was not seeking Him, nor did he want Christianity to be true. He reached a point where the books he read, the conversations he had, the thoughts that went through his head kept pushing him closer and closer to the unwanted belief that Jesus Christ was the Son of God and the source of salvation and that he would have to respond to Him one way or another.

Lewis associated Christianity with "ugly architecture, ugly music, and bad poetry," but he also resisted it because of his own "deep-seated hatred of authority, my monstrous individualism, my lawlessness. No word in my vocabulary expressed deeper hatred than the word *Interference*. But Christianity placed at the center what then seemed to me a transcendental Interferer."

Despite Lewis's aversion to divine meddling, God the Interferer hit him from all directions. One influence was the books he read. Just as Collins was profoundly influenced by Lewis's *Mere Christianity*, so Lewis himself was knocked off stride by reading George MacDonald, G. K. Chesterton, and others. He wrote,

> In reading Chesterton, as in reading MacDonald, I did not know what I was letting myself in for. A young man who wishes to remain a sound Atheist cannot be too careful of his reading. There are traps everywhere—"Bibles laid open, millions of surprises," as Herbert says, "fine nets and stratagems." God is, if I may say it, very unscrupulous.

Later, his encounters with God in books only escalated. He found himself most drawn to writers with a strong Christian or at least religious bent. He had often dismissed the Christian element by saying that these writers were good except for their Christianity, but with so many of those good writers piling up, how long could he continue that? "Indeed, I must have been blind as a bat not to have seen, long before, the ludicrous contradiction between my theory of life and my actual experiences as a reader."[7]

With other converts we have seen that once God pursues people, they seem to find Him wherever they turn. Linda Freeman couldn't even go to a restaurant in the middle of the night without a stranger approaching her about Jesus. Lauren Winner, looking back on the years leading up to her conversion, saw her path strewn with clues of God's presence. Anne Lamott described her movement toward faith as not a leap but rather a stagger from one safe "lily pad" to another from childhood until the time of her conversion. C. S. Lewis likewise found that not only were the books he read moving him closer to belief in God, but so were the people he talked to, even though some were atheists and had no intention of leading him to Christ.

One night, for instance, during the period when God, Lewis's "Adversary, began to make His final moves," he had a conversation with "the hardest boiled of all the atheists I ever knew," who sat in his room and "remarked that the evidence for the historicity of the gospels was really surprisingly good. 'Rum thing,' he went on. 'All that stuff of Frazer's about the Dying God. It almost looks as if it had really happened once.'"

On top of all the other conversations and all the books that had been shaking his resistance to Christianity, this comment was "shattering" to Lewis. "If he, the cynic of cynics, the toughest of the toughs, were not—as I would have put it—'safe,' where could I turn? Was there then no escape?"

Lewis did not escape. After all the thinking and reading and conversation leading up to his moment of decision, by the time that moment came, it seemed as if there was no real decision left to make. Although Lewis still did not want it to be so, God's existence and presence were by then undeniable. He wrote,

> You must picture me alone in that room in Magdalen, night after night, feeling, whenever my mind lifted even for a second from my work, the steady, unrelenting approach of Him whom I so earnestly desired not to meet. That which I greatly feared had at last come upon me. In the Trinity Term of 1929 I gave in, and admitted that God was God, and knelt and prayed: perhaps, that night, the most dejected and reluctant convert in all England.[8]

That was his conversion to theism only. His final move to Christianity would come only after more searching, including crucial conversations with friends like J. R. R. Tolkien and Hugo Dyson. Now that he believed in God, he had to seek answers to the questions "Where has religion reached its true maturity?" and "Where, if anywhere, have the hints of all paganism been fulfilled?" Other religions fell short in various ways. Only Christianity remained a possibility for Lewis, and the more he studied it and the more God closed in, the closer he came to belief.

"If ever a myth had become fact, had been incarnated, it would be just like this," wrote Lewis. "And nothing else in all literature was just like this. Myths were like it in one way. Histories were like it in another. But nothing was simply like it."

Lewis's moment of conversion was nothing like the dramatic and emotional events we've seen with other converts. It happened during a ride to the zoo. "When we set out I did not believe that Jesus Christ is the Son of God, and when we reached the zoo I did," wrote Lewis.[9] That's it. No bright light, so singing of angels, no tears of gratitude and emotional release. C. S. Lewis was now a Christian, and he would go on to write books that would lead countless others to Jesus Christ in much the same way as he had reached Him.

"A Stranger Among Strangers in a Strange Land"

Although Francis Collins and C. S. Lewis went through a long process of conversion, they were still young men when they turned to Christ. Journalist and documentary filmmaker Malcolm Muggeridge, who shared with those men a probing mind and skeptical outlook, did not join a church until he was in his eighties. He wrote, "In my own case, conversion has been more a series of happenings than one single dramatic one. I have a memory of occasions so sharp that they brought a new and lasting dimension of faith into my life."[10]

Muggeridge's conversion story differs in many respects from those of Lewis and Collins, whose conversions seemed to follow a somewhat more linear, though complex, path, as one objection to Christianity after another fell away, and they were left with little choice but to believe in Christianity. Muggeridge tells of dramatic moments throughout his life when he came right up to the edge of belief, only to back away at the last minute.

He grew up in a family who believed God was irrelevant. His father and his friends believed that political progress, rather than Christianity, would bring about a more loving and peaceful world. The young Malcolm shared his father's idealistic dream of the possibilities of political progress, but even then he couldn't get away from his interest in Jesus of the New Testament. He secretly acquired a Bible of his own, covered it with a brown paper cover as if it were a forbidden book, marked the passages that moved him most, and even took it to bed with him at night.

As he grew up, went to college, and became a journalist covering places like the Stalin-era Soviet Union, Muggeridge became disillusioned with his father's faith in the power of political progress to change the world. But if political progress were not the answer, then what was? Muggeridge's decades-long search for God was filled with the kind of foreshadowing evident in the lives of so many other converts as he moved tantalizingly close to belief without making a full commitment. God the Pursuer kept after him through the years of this movement toward and away from faith.

One of the many times Muggeridge moved close to conversion before shrinking back was a day during World War II as he lay on his cot in the midst of his fellow soldiers. As he lay there trying to will himself to be the first one to get into the shower facilities, he contemplated God's love and the love among human beings, and he asked himself directly what he truly believed. He immediately began reciting the words he used to say at Cambridge in College

Chapel: "I believe in God, the Father Almighty, maker of Heaven and Earth, and in Jesus Christ His only Son, our Lord."

But did he really believe it? He wanted to, he thought he did, but he also doubted. Although he had "an impulse then and there to kneel down by his bed and proclaim his faith," cowardice stepped in, and instead, he merely cursed himself for having lingered in his cot so long that he would not be first in line for the showers.[11]

Muggeridge's story is peppered with these "almost conversions," but one powerful turning point happened during the war when he worked for his country as a spy against the Germans and Italians in Mozambique. He describes this period as the lowest point of his life—but also the most decisive. Part of his job involved gathering information in the bars and cafes that were part of the squalid nightlife of the capital city. After one such depressing, alcohol-soaked night, he decided to commit suicide.

Close to the bars he had just frequented, he took off his clothes and waded out into the ocean. Once he reached deeper water, he began swimming out as far as he could. He swam far out, beyond his depth, and then an easy feeling came over him since the decision was now made. His body trembled. He sank under the water, came back up, lay on his back, and floated.

That night could have been the end of Muggeridge's story, but instead, it became the beginning of his "spiritual adolescence." Suddenly, without thinking about it or knowing why, he began swimming back to shore. He kept his eyes on the lights of the bars on shore. Although he was so tired he wasn't sure he could make it back, an overwhelming joy and ecstasy came over him. As he later described his thoughts at that moment (and writing about himself in the third person),

> *In some mysterious way it became clear to him that there was no darkness, only the possibility of losing sight of a light which shone eternally;* that our clumsy appetites are no more than the blind reaching of a newborn child after the teat

through which to suck the milk of life; that our sufferings, our affliction, are part of a drama—an essential, even an ecstatic, part—endlessly revolving round the two great propositions of good and evil, light and darkness.

Muggeridge made it back to shore, but he did not convert to Christianity that night. From that moment on, however, "all his values and pursuits were going to undergo a total transformation—from the carnal towards the spiritual; from the immediate, the now, towards the everlasting, the eternal." His spiritual journey continued to be characterized by these moments of illumination, of almost reaching conversion, followed by a backing away into more doubt and searching. Even when he finally joined a church near the end of his life, he said, "I have to confess, then, that I can only fitfully believe, can believe no creed wholly, have had no all-sufficing moment of illumination."[12]

A conversion story like Muggeridge's lacks the simplicity of the dramatic, once-and-for-all transforming moment of many others we have seen, but it may be an encouragement to people whose spiritual journeys are "untidy" and meandering. Muggeridge's story and the conversions of people like Francis Collins and C. S. Lewis offer hope for people who squirm at the thought of belief but who nevertheless feel the tug of God and can't quite get away from the conviction that He does exist and that He is in loving pursuit of them. The path of these converts is often blocked by intellectual barriers, but as those barriers fall, one by one, they see that the path, to their surprise, leads to Jesus Christ and to eternity. Conversion, however, does not obliterate doubt. In fact, as we'll explore in the next chapter, it often ushers it in.

Go to www.beaconhillbooks.com/go/godinpursuit for a free downloadable Study Guide that includes questions for deeper personal reflection as well as activities for use in a small-group setting.

NINE

Slightly Beyond the Tipping Point
Attacks of Doubt, the Impulse to Serve

For many Christians the aftermath of conversion is one of the happiest times of their lives. Many report a sense of relief, the feeling of a burden lifted, a particular closeness of the Holy Spirit. Many say their joy is so obvious that their friends notice that something is different about them even before they speak a word about what has happened to them. Many feel an urgent enthusiasm about spiritual matters and have trouble understanding why long-time Christians seem so blasé about their faith.

Joy as a result of conversion is something I would expect, but I found another impulse following many conversions that was more of a surprise: an attack of intense doubt and insecurity. Once the powerful emotion that often—but not always—accompanies conversion fades, the new Christian may wonder, *Was the experience real? Can it be trusted? Are there other explanations for what happened?* Like Sara Miles, who tried to explain away her conversion after her dramatic first Communion, many other new converts are tempted to doubt their salvation.

113

Conversion Is Often Accompanied By an Attack of Doubt

One of the most famous and influential conversions in history was that of John Wesley, the founder of Methodism. After years of trying to gain his salvation by his own efforts of trying to keep God's law "inward and outward to the utmost of my power," Wesley finally realized that he could not achieve union with God through his own righteousness and self-denial. Only through faith in Christ would salvation come.

One night Wesley went "very unwillingly" to a meeting in Aldersgate Street, where someone was reading Luther's preface to the book of Romans. Wesley wrote,

> About a quarter before nine, while he was describing the change which God works in the heart through faith in Christ, I felt my heart strangely warmed. I felt I did trust in Christ, Christ alone for salvation; and an assurance was given me that He had taken away *my* sins, even *mine*, and saved *me* from the law of sin and death.

That would be a beautiful place to stop the story, and Wesley's "heart strangely warmed" has inspired millions. But what is less well-known is that he was plagued with doubts almost from that same moment. After praying and testifying to everyone there about what had happened to him, he says that "it was not long before the enemy suggested, 'This cannot be faith; for where is thy joy?'" After returning home that night, he was "much buffeted with temptations" that "returned again and again." The next day, "Jesus, Master" was in his heart and mouth the moment he awakened, but it was not long before "the enemy injected a fear: 'If thou dost believe, why is there not a more sensible change?'"[1]

The doubts Wesley confronted were serious but not nearly as intense as those endured by John Bunyan, who later became famous for writing one of the great bestsellers of all time, *The Pilgrim's Progress*. For months and even years at a stretch, Bunyan veered between hope of salvation and despair that he was lost. At one point in the midst of this spiritual despondency, Bunyan decided to pray to God even though he feared that in his case such prayer might be futile. In his prayer he said that Satan had told him that neither God's "mercy, nor Christ's blood is sufficient to save my soul." He asked God if he should believe that or if he should believe that God could and would save him.

As he prayed, the scripture came his mind—"O man, great is thy faith." He could have taken this as a confirmation of his faith, but he said he was

> not able to believe this, that this was a prayer of faith, till almost six months after; for I could not think that I had faith, or that there should be a word for me to act faith on; therefore I should still be, as sticking in the jaws of desperation, and went mourning up and down in a sad condition.

No matter how powerful Bunyan's encounter with God, it was usually followed by a bout of insecurity or hopelessness. At one point his spiritual agony over his salvation seemed to ease when the words from Scripture, "My grace is sufficient," darted into his mind. He said,

> By these words I was sustained, yet not without exceeding conflicts, for the space of seven or eight weeks; for my peace would be in it, and out, sometimes twenty times a day, comfort now, and trouble presently; peace now, and before I could go a furlong, as full of fear and guilt as ever heart could hold; and this was not only now and then, but my whole seven weeks' experience.[2]

How did these men, who would go on to lead countless others to Christ, overcome their own insecurities about their salvation? Fending off these doubts was not easy, especially for Bunyan, but both men learned to identify the lies that were at the base of each doubt, and then to refute those lies with scripture and with their faith in Jesus Christ that went deeper than their fluctuations in emotions. Wesley was attacked with doubt because he didn't feel the overflow of joy that often accompanies conversion, but then he realized that "as to the transports of joy . . . God sometimes giveth, sometimes withholdeth them, according to the counsels of His own will." As for the fear that his conversion was suspect because there was not a more "sensible change" in him, Wesley said, "I answered (yet not I), 'That I know not. But this I know, I have 'now peace with God.' And I sin not today, and Jesus my Master has forbid me to take thought for the morrow."[3]

For Bunyan, the end of his tormented wavering between doubt and faith came only when he stopped focusing on his own attempts at pleasing God and his own unreliable feelings and realized that his salvation depended on Christ alone. "I also saw moreover," he later wrote, "that it was not my good frame of heart that made my righteousness better, nor yet my bad frame that made my righteousness worse; for my righteousness was Jesus Christ himself, 'the same yesterday, today and forever.'"[4]

Half the battle of confronting the attack of doubts at the point of conversion is simply knowing that such an attack is a common part of the experience for many people. This inner turmoil does not invalidate the spiritual transformation that has taken place. John Wesley wrote that as he struggled with the meaning of his conversion, he was tempted by the question "But is not any sort of fear a proof that thou dost not believe?" He responded, "I desired my Master to answer for me, and opened His Book upon those words of St. Paul, 'Without were fightings, within were fears.' Then, inferred I, well may fears be within me; but I must go on, and tread them under my feet."[5]

Salvation Is Instant. Transformation May Take Time

Transformation is part of conversion. Some people say that when they turned to Christ, many aspects of their attitudes and lifestyles changed immediately. For others, however, the transformation of old habits, desires, and spiritual struggles is a more gradual process. Their lives have changed direction at conversion, but it may take time to escape the grip of certain behaviors that have held them captive. The danger for some new converts is that if they lack patience and lack trust in God to transform them, they may conclude that these early failures mean their conversion was not real, and they may fall away from it. But with love and support from the Christian community, these new believers over time will reach a greater level of spiritual maturity

In *The Varieties of Religious Experience,* William James tells of the son of a clergyman in England in the late nineteenth century who wanted nothing to do with his father's church. He was well-educated, with a degree from Oxford, but had a bad drinking problem and sometimes would be drunk for a week at a time. He sometimes felt remorse about his drinking, but up to age 33 he said he "never had a desire to reform on religious grounds."

His conversion came as a big surprise to him. It happened while he was alone in his bedroom reading a book a friend had asked him to critique purely on literary, not religious, grounds. He said, "It was here God met me face to face, and I shall never forget the meeting."

In his reading he came across the verse of Scripture that reads, "He that hath the Son hath life eternal, he that hath not the Son hath not life." He had read this verse many times before, but now he was "in God's presence and my attention was absolutely 'soldered' on to this verse, and I was not allowed to proceed with the book till I had fairly considered what these words really involved."

A great sorrow swept over him, because he knew his "doom was sealed" and he "was lost to a certainty." But then, "there crept in upon me so gently, so lovingly, so unmistakably, a way of escape, and what was it after all? The old, old story over again, told in the simplest way: 'There is no name under heaven whereby ye can be saved except that of the Lord Jesus Christ.'" The turning point for this man was realizing that only Jesus could save him, and he became a

Christian that day. He says that within twenty-four hours his whole village had heard about his astounding conversion.

This young man was transformed, but despite this powerful conversion story, his struggles were not over. The next day he went out to help with the harvest in the hayfield, and "not having made any promise to God to abstain or drink in moderation only, I took too much and came home drunk." This drunkenness on his first full day of being a Christian was devastating to the man's sister, who was heartbroken and cried and lamented that he had converted but had fallen away instantly.

Although he regretted his behavior, however, this new convert said that even in his intoxicated state, he "knew that God's work begun in me was not going to be wasted."[6] His conversion was real. God was working in him, and he did eventually overcome his drinking problem. He continued to pray and to surrender himself fully to God. Surrender was the key. Just as he realized at the point of conversion that only God could save him, he now also realized that only God could transform him.

For many people, this work takes more time and struggle than some new converts or some fellow Christians think it should. Many problems may still require professional help, and new converts need to be bathed in encouragement from fellow believers. But the fact that spiritual battles over old habits, behaviors, and addictions still must be fought after conversion does not mean the conversion was invalid. God has begun His transforming work and will continue it as people trust Him and surrender their lives to Him.

Sometimes Doubts About Conversion Spring from Other People, Even Christians

New converts to Christianity, already dealing with the enormity of the change that has occurred in their lives, are particularly vulnerable to the reactions of other people. Those fears about what other people will think may add to the inner insecurities new Christians already feel about the leaps they've just taken. We've already seen that in a number of conversion stories. When converting to Christianity in a Muslim culture, Ziya Meral had to take into account the high cost of the disapproval of family, friends, and his community, which might deprive him of marriage, a livelihood, and many other fundamentals of life. Wiretapper Jim Vaus would have to worry about how his mob bosses and associates might react to the threat they felt from his dangerous turn to Christianity. Anne Lamott, Brian Welch, and Joe Eszterhas all faced resistance to their conversions from longtime friends or business associates or fans.

Even in communities more supportive of Christianity, the responses of other people can shake the confidence of the new convert. Charles Finney's conversion in the 1820s in a strong Christian community was emotional and dramatic, as he sensed the Holy Spirit descending upon him in "waves and waves of liquid love; for I could not express it in any other way. It seemed like the very breath of God. I can recollect distinctly that it seemed to fan me, like immense wings." Yet despite the power of that experience, Finney was thrown into uncertainty about his conversion later that day when he told an elder of the church about it. For reasons Finney could not fathom, the elder broke into laughter as he heard the story.

Later, when Finney was alone, this inexplicable laughter plagued the young man. "Did he not think that I was under a delusion, or crazy? A cloud seemed to shut in over me; I had no hold upon anything in which I could rest. . . . Notwithstanding the baptism I had received, this temptation so obscured my view that I went to bed without feeling sure that my peace was made with God."

Finney and these other converts held on to their relationship with Jesus Christ despite the costs and dangers and insecurities. The power of the Holy Spirit in their lives was simply stronger than any of those other forces. Ultimately, they could not deny the transformation that had taken place in them. Finney went to bed with a cloud of doubt hanging over him, but he awoke with a strong sense of the Holy Spirit's presence in his life.

This renewed confidence was accompanied by what he considered "a gentle reproof" as "the Spirit seemed to say to me, 'Will you doubt? Will you doubt?' I cried, 'No! I will not doubt; I cannot doubt.' He then cleared the subject up so much to my mind that it was in fact impossible for me to doubt that the Spirit of God had taken possession of my soul."[7]

Young converts might expect that older believers would be thrilled that new and enthusiastic Christians have now joined them in their faith, but that's not always the case. Sometimes new Christians enter the body of believers with such zeal that it makes the more settled and complacent church members uncomfortable.

Albert Schweitzer tells a funny yet sad story of the response he got from family members and fellow Christians when he decided to become a missionary doctor in Africa. Although he would go on to win the Nobel Peace Prize and be recognized around the world for his dedicated Christian service, his calling at first brought mockery and resistance from many of the Christians closest to him.

Schweitzer's radical decision at age thirty was to leave a comfortable academic position and to pursue a riskier endeavor to which he believed Christ was calling him. Up to that time he had dedicated himself to philosophy and theology and music, but from that time forward he determined he would devote himself

> to the direct service of humanity. Many a time already had I tried to settle what meaning lay hidden for me in the saying of Jesus 'Whoever would save his life shall lose it, and whoever shall lose his life for My sake and the Gospels shall save it.' Now the answer was found. In addition to the outward, I now had inward happiness.

How could any fellow Christian argue with such a resolve? Schweitzer's family and friends didn't mind his Christian commitment in terms of his *beliefs*—those were safe and commendable—but for him to actually step out, leave a successful academic career, spend years in medical school, and then head off to some far-flung place to serve, as they termed them, "savages"—was taking things too far. They came up with many objections to try to deter him from his plan. Why had he not consulted them before deciding on such a radical course of action? Why not let someone else serve the Africans? As Schweitzer recalled, they told him that "work among savages I ought to leave to those who would not thereby be compelled to leave gifts and acquirements in science and art unused."

He was discouraged by having to fight so hard to make Christians understand his motives for wanting to follow Christ. "In the many verbal duels which I had to fight, as a weary opponent, with people who passed for Christians, it moved me strangely to see them so far from perceiving that the effort to serve the love preached by Jesus may sweep a man into a new course of life." Instead of admiring his deep commitment, they tried to dismiss his decision by blaming it on some sort of character flaw. Some accused him of conceit. Some blamed "unfortunate love experiences" for his resolve to run off to the jungle and serve as a doctor. He said others regarded him "as a precocious young man, not quite right in the head, and treated me correspondingly with affectionate mockery."[8]

Schweitzer's calling burned so strongly in him that he followed it in the face of this opposition from other Christians and many other obstacles that were put in his path along the way. He went through medical school and traveled to remote western Africa, where he established and served as a physician in a hospital that served thousands of patients. Throughout his remarkable life he continued to make other important contributions in other fields that interested him—music, philosophy, and theology. Like Wesley, Finney, and the others, Schweitzer refused to allow his own doubts or the doubts of others keep him from serving the Lord who had such a powerful grip on him.

Sitting in a Pew Is Not Enough: The Impulse to Serve

Just as a bout of insecurity is common in the moments or days following conversion, I found another impulse to be even more widespread in dozens of conversion stories: the impulse to serve others. Often this urge comes in the form of wanting to tell others about Christ in order to bring them into relationship with Him, but it takes other forms as well. In some cases the person can act on this calling immediately, while for other people, such as Schweitzer, it takes years for the details to come together. What most converts seem to sense immediately, however, even if no one teaches it to them, is that their conversion is not simply a matter between them and Jesus Christ alone. It will have a profound effect on how they relate to everyone around them.

In many of the people whose conversion stories we have already looked at, the compulsion to reach out to others was strong. Following her conversion, Sara Miles felt the desire to feed people. As she explained in a PBS interview, what she discovered when she was converted during her first Communion was that

> the requirement of faith turned out not to be believing in a doctrine, or knowing how to behave in a church, or being the right kind of person, or being raised correctly, or repeating the rituals. The requirement for faith seemed to be hunger. It was the hunger that I had always had and the willingness to be fed by something I didn't understand.[9]

Now Miles is director of the Food Pantry at San Francisco's St. Gregory of Nyssa Episcopal Church, where she and her volunteers distribute five or six tons of groceries every week to anyone who needs them.

As noted earlier, following his conversion and his imprisonment for Watergate crimes, Chuck Colson felt the impulse to reach out to prisoners with the gospel. He started Prison Fellowship, the largest prison outreach in the world, with more than 50,000 volunteers who minister in every state and more than 100 nations. When

Mary Kay Beard went from being a criminal on the FBI's Ten Most Wanted list to being a convert to Christianity in prison, she didn't wait for her freedom before she started reaching out to others. She organized a Bible study in prison so she could share her faith. After she got out, she started the Angel Tree ministry, now part of Colson's Prison Fellowship, which ministers to the family members of people in prison. Through Angel Tree, more than 12,000 churches now give Christmas gifts each year to more than half a million children. The ministry also has mentoring and camping programs for the children of prisoners.

For many, the desire to serve others springs not from something they've been taught they *should* do, but from the love that floods into their own lives in their new relationship with Jesus Christ. C. F. Andrews, who became an advocate for exploited laborers around the world and was a friend of Mahatma Ghandi, had a powerful and emotional conversion to Christianity. He wrote that Christ's "grace and love flood my whole being," and in the days that followed, the "different world of light and love and peace" made him love everyone he met. This new love did not confine itself to sentimental feelings. Instead, Andrews said the "effect of this inflow of the Spirit, which came from Christ, was immediately to send me among the poor. Though, up to that time, I was quite unacquainted with the work of service in Christ's name, an inner compulsion seemed to drive me towards it; and all through my life the impulse to surrender all for Christ's sake and to find Him among those who are in need has been present with me so strongly that sooner or later everything has had to give way before it."[10] His compulsion sent him to laborers in India, South Africa, and many other places across the world.

Some converts we've already looked at felt the call to preach. John Wesley, Jonathan Edwards, Charles Spurgeon Charles Finney, the apostle Paul, and others spread the gospel to millions through their preaching. Others felt a particular call to the poor, to prisoners, to exploited workers, or others. Not everyone serves in a way that becomes so well-known, of course. For every one of these prominent converts, there are thousands of others who live quieter lives of service and spread the gospel to family members, friends, neighbors, and strangers right around them.

The transformation that happens as part of becoming a follower of Christ will take many different forms, but conversion is not something that happens only inside a person. It will pour out to others in some way. As Peace put it, "Unless faith spills over into life, it is merely an intellectual game. So too conversion. It is merely an idea or experience until it reveals itself by the new way one lives. Unless there is transformation, there is no conversion."[11]

Go to www.beaconhillbooks.com/go/godinpursuit for a free downloadable Study Guide that includes questions for deeper personal reflection as well as activities for use in a small-group setting.

Far Beyond the Tipping Point
The Dance of Doubt and Faith

To be spiritually alive is to be in spiritual danger. The leap of faith into conversion is a jump across one hurdle but by no means the final one. For the spiritually alive Christian, doubt and spiritual struggles continue and may even intensify, though in different forms and accompanied by different questions than in pre-conversion days.

As many of the conversion stories in this book have shown, God often appears in people's lives well before they're searching for Him or wanting Him or before they've done their homework to prepare for Him. Malcolm Muggeridge was trying to kill himself when God showed up. Linda Freeman was taking a cigarette break. While this is one of the most thrilling aspects of how God reaches people, it is also one of the most dangerous.

Why dangerous? These individuals haven't yet had the time or inclination to consider all the possible objections to Christianity. They haven't worked through all the theological, intellectual, and philosophical difficulties. God reaches them, they respond in repentance and acceptance, and they enter into the faith. That doesn't mean they'll never have to struggle with the tough questions. It means only that their time of questioning has been postponed.

If God operated in a polite and logical way, people who come to faith would have the chance to start at the beginning. They would file in like earnest graduate students and start with questions such as "Does God exist?" Then they would move on to "If He does exist, is Christianity the true manifestation of Him?" Once these and a long list of other questions were answered to their satisfaction, they would convert.

Some converts do get the opportunity to ask many of the tough questions before they turn to Christ. C. S. Lewis and Francis Collins, for instance, studied various religions, read some key books, discussed and debated theology with friends and experts. Far more often, though, when God finds them, people are simply too surprised or too young or inexperienced or unfamiliar with spiritual issues to even know what questions to ask. At this point they may know only enough to realize that God's loving Spirit is drawing them toward Him, that they are separated from Him and they need forgiveness through Jesus Christ to make themselves right with God. They respond. They invite Him in, sometimes praying in terminology so unsophisticated and personal that the experts might have trouble recognizing it as the very theology they espouse.

In the glow of new faith in Jesus Christ, some new Christians may feel that disbelief has been put behind them forever. Months or years may go by without any serious jolt to their faith, but then the crisis hits. The doubt may present itself in many forms. For some Christians, it may show up as identifiable questions: Why has so much evil been carried out in the name of religion? How could a good God allow people to go to hell? Why isn't one religion as valid a path to God as any other?

The doubt may creep into their lives in ways that go deeper than words, as the Holy Spirit seems to fade out of their lives, as despair threatens, as boredom overwhelms. The crisis of doubt

may be triggered by circumstances—a devastating career blow, the death of someone precious, the sudden deterioration of one's health. Disillusionment with the church or many other causes may trigger a faith crisis.

The outcome of these periods can be devastating. Some believers leave the church. Some abandon their belief in Christ. In *Finding Faith, Losing Faith*, Scot McKnight and Hauna Ondrey tell of many Christians who gave up their faith after a crisis of doubt. One of those, Dan Barker, a former Christian minister and evangelist, told them,

> I did not lose my faith. I gave it up purposely. The motivation that drove me into the ministry is the same that drove me out. I have always wanted to *know*. Even as a child I fervently pursued the truth. . . . For years I went through intense inner conflict. . . . I would cry out to God for answers. . . . I kept trusting that God would someday come through. He never did. The only proposed answer was faith, and I gradually grew to dislike the smell of that word. I finally realized that faith is a cop-out, a defeat—an admission that the truths of religion are unknowable through evidence and reason. . . . It is only undemonstrable assertions that require the suspension of reason, and weak ideas that require faith. I just lost faith in faith.[1]

Barker became an atheist.

In *Quitting Church*, Julia Duin investigates why so many American Christians are dropping out of churches. Among the many reasons she found, she writes,

> Many people I encountered were disappointed or perplexed in some way with God. They'd been Christians for more than a decade, and some had experienced serious suffering. The more honest ones admitted something was not working in their Christian faith. They were not connecting with God as to the reason for their sorrows; in fact God seemed to be confounding their prayers. Their churches were useless in giving meaning-

ful counsel, and if these people brought up their concerns in a Bible study, their doubts and anger toward God were frowned on by others in the group.[2]

Some of the people she wrote about traded traditional church for a home Bible study or some other form of worship, but others abandoned their relationship with Christ entirely.

The destruction of one's faith, however, is not the inevitable outcome of a crisis of doubt. On the contrary, weathering such a crisis by confronting the tough questions can be exhilarating. Christians may emerge more in love with God than ever, their understanding deepened, their faith more solid.

Believers don't *seek* these dark times, nor do they welcome them. These periods of spiritual turmoil may be like a marriage rocked by the upheaval of financial chaos or the pain of deep disagreement. If the couple survives, they may emerge on the other side with a deeper commitment to one another, believing that if they can survive that, they can survive anything. They come through with a love that is deeper but less naive, less giddy but more unshakable.

Fear Indifference More than Doubt

Doubt is what many Christians fear, but in fact they should be much more afraid of long, stagnant periods when the spiritual waters are so calm that no doubts ever arise. What they think of as spiritual stability may in fact be a sign that their faith is so dormant it's too dead to produce any doubt—or much belief either. Although I know of some Christians who have given up their faith because of intellectual objections they can't get beyond, I know of far more people who have lost their faith without ever struggling with doubt. Doubt doesn't touch them because they live their spiritual lives on such a superficial basis that any doubt that comes up is kept as amorphous and free-floating as their faith itself. They don't truly engage in either one. They drift away from doubt just as easily as they coast along in their faith.

The mindset of spiritual drifters—who may be long-time Christians and stalwarts of the church—may work something like this: They converted long ago, so that little piece of spiritual business is taken care of. Now their unstated goal is to float through their spiritual lives with as little fuss as possible. They go to church regularly, sing the songs, hear the sermons, put some money into the offering plate, and try not to get roped into volunteering for too many ministry projects. They read Bible verses when the situation calls for it, such as during a Sunday School lesson, but they feel no great need to study it on their own. After all, they know the basic message. The rest is just details. They pray if the notion strikes but see no need to devote much energy to it. God already knows how they feel and what they're thinking, so why belabor it?

They believe. It's settled. They don't *intend* for the fervor of faith to fade. It's just that life flings countless demands from every direction, and those obligations of family, work, and getting through the day drain away the energy that might otherwise be spent meditating on scripture or praying to God or serving others or tracking down answers to some nagging spiritual doubt. These well-intentioned, drifting believers pay homage to their faith more than they really live it. There is the spiritual realm, and there is real life, and the two gradually drift farther apart.

These Christians become the walking dead long before they would ever realize or acknowledge that their spiritual life is in trouble. Eventually some of them stick with Christianity only because it would take more energy to walk away—there would be all that explaining to do.

Under these shaky circumstances, it might take only one puff of air to push these Christians out of the church altogether. They may move to a new city and "never find the right church," or there may be a change of pastor or a switch in the style of worship music or a church conflict that gives them the excuse they need to get out inconspicuously.

Faith is a living, breathing entity. Doubt, far from being an indication that your faith is weak, can instead be a sign that you're still breathing. Doubt may even be necessary for faith's survival. As Timothy Keller, author of *The Reason for God*, puts it,

> A faith without some doubt is like a human body without any antibodies in it. People who blithely go through life too busy or indifferent to ask hard questions about why they believe as they do will find themselves defenseless against either the experience of tragedy or the probing questions of a smart skeptic. A person's faith can collapse almost overnight if she has failed over the years to listen patiently to her own doubts, which should only be discarded after long reflection.[3]

Crisis of Doubt May Lead to Spiritual Triumph

Doubt and faith are cyclical, but not in any predictable way, not so that you could write it out in a diagram. Issues that we may have skimmed over before as irrelevant or thought were settled may suddenly arise to grip our soul. Even if we engage them now, they may return in a different form later as we approach the questions from a deeper point in our faith.

It's similar to what happens when I teach literature to college students. When students come across a writer in my course who in high school they had considered dull or confusing, they are often surprised at how much they enjoy that writer's works now. Even though the writer hasn't changed, the student reads the author from a higher level of maturity and with a wider context of other works the student has studied since that time.

In my own reading of authors I teach year after year, I'm amazed by the new ways I'm able to see them as I continue studying their works. Writers like Mark Twain and Emily Dickinson and William Faulkner offer insights I had missed or didn't have the life experiences to appreciate as an undergraduate. Similarly, some authors who had seemed so brilliant when I was a teenager now come across as shallow and predictable.

At certain points in life, a doubt-producing question such as how a good God could allow suffering may seem like little more than an abstract, nitpicky question for philosophers and theologians. It is remote from your own daily relationship with Jesus Christ. But at other times, in the midst of your own crisis of suffering or as you watch someone else go through deep pain, the question may shake you to the core.

Regardless of the conclusions you may come to about the question at any particular point, the question is likely to come back in a different form with a different degree of relevance at another time. This cycle of questioning and deepening your understanding may happen not only on particular questions, but also with regard to your overall faith itself.

Barbara Brown Taylor describes her own "seasons" of faith this way:

> Like every believer I know, my search for real life has led me through at least three distinct seasons of faith, not once or twice, but over and over again. Jesus called them finding life, losing life, and finding life again, with the paradoxical promise that finders will be losers while those who lose their lives for His sake will wind up finding them again. In Greek the word is *psyche*, meaning not only "life" but also the conscious self, the personality, the soul. You do not have to die in order to discover the truth of this teaching, in other words. You only need to lose track of who you are, or who you thought you were supposed to be, so that you end up lying flat on the dirt floor basement of your heart. Do this, Jesus says, and you will live.[4]

This cycle does not lead Christians back to where they started any more than coming back to a classic author leads the literature student back to the same reading experience he or she had before. The student, now more mature and experienced than the first time around, approaches the author with as much to gain as if he or she had never read him, and the Christian who comes back to a "settled" issue arrives with as much at stake is if the question had never before been asked. Sometimes the return to the issue will be easier than the first time, a mere refinement of earlier lessons learned. At other times the very survival of the Christian's faith may be at risk. Although many may dread or may even refuse to enter such dangerous spiritual territory, the place of gravest doubt may also become the place of greatest spiritual triumph, leaving the believer with a richer understanding of God than ever would have been possible in the more tranquil spiritual days.

Mother Teresa: Clinging to Jesus in the Midst of Darkness

One of the most admired Christians of the twentieth century was Mother Teresa, who founded the Missionaries of Charity to serve the poor in Calcutta, India. Her order now serves the poorest of the poor in dozens of countries across the world. She was awarded the Nobel Peace Prize in 1979 and was given many other honors throughout her life, but she was best known for her humble, Christlike spirit and her devotion to serving the sick and the poor and the downtrodden in Jesus' name.

If anyone was assumed to have a close connection to Jesus, it was Mother Teresa, but the 2007 publication of some of her private writings, compiled in a book called *Come Be My Light*, drew great attention because they revealed that for almost fifty years of her life, Mother Teresa did not sense the presence of God. Although she had given herself over to Christ and never wavered in that commitment, she felt as if He had withdrawn His presence from her. Her doubt and bewilderment were focused not so much on whether God existed but on why He had seemingly pushed her away when she so longed for the close relationship to God that she had once known. She revealed this sense of God's absence only to a few close spiritual advisors, and her papers, which she never wanted published, were not made public until ten years after her death.

The absence of God's loving spirit was all the more painful because she had sensed him so powerfully as a young woman. Her love for Jesus was so intense that in 1942 she did something quite special: "I made a vow to God, binding under [pain of] mortal sin, to give God anything that He may ask, 'Not to refuse Him anything.'" She remained true to that vow, not only then, when the Holy Spirit was very close, but also in later years, when He seemed far off.

Much later, feeling cut off from God, even though her ministry was prospering, she wrote, "My own soul remains in deep darkness and desolation. No I don't complain—let Him do with me whatever He wants."[5] She was determined not to make her own commitment to God contingent on any particular way that He may nor may not manifest himself to her. But early on, at the time she made the vow, she had heard Jesus' voice within her calling her toward the ministry to the poor in Calcutta.

Given this close connection to Jesus, how bewildering it was for Mother Teresa when that voice and presence withdrew and was replaced by silence and a feeling of rejection, even though she was following God's calling as best she knew how. In one letter she describes her dilemma as

> this continual longing for God—which gives me that pain deep down in my heart. Darkness is such that I really do not see neither with my mind nor with my reason. . . . The place of God in my soul is blank. . . . There is no God in me. . . . When the pain of longing is so great . . . I just long and long for God . . . and then it is that I feel . . . He does not want me . . . He is not there.[6]

Could such a crisis of doubt and pain serve any spiritual purpose? Brian Kolodiejchuk, who edited *Come Be My Light*, wrote that at first Mother Teresa "attributed this absence to her sinfulness and weakness, concluding that the darkness was purification of her imperfections."[7] But as time went on, and as she worked with her spiritual advisors, she began to see it from a broader perspective. Her own pain became a way of identifying with and attaching herself to the pain of Jesus on the Cross. She wrote, "What are you doing, my God, to one so small? When you asked to imprint your Passion on my heart—is this the answer?"[8]

Her pain also became a way of connecting to the poor people her ministry served. As Kolodiejchuk explains,

> Her darkness was an identification with those she served: she was drawn mystically into the deep pain they experienced as a result of feeling unwanted and rejected and, above all, by living without faith in God. Years before, she had been willing to offer herself as a victim for even one soul. She was now called to be united in the pain, not only with one soul, but with a multitude of souls that suffered in this terrible darkness.

This understanding of the spiritual function of her pain acted as a kind of tipping point for Mother Teresa in coming to terms with her spiritual crisis. One of her spiritual advisors wrote,

> It was the redeeming experience of her life when she realized that the night of her heart was the special share she had in Jesus' passion. . . . Thus we see that the darkness was actually the mysterious link that united her to Jesus. It is the contact of intimate longing for God.[9]

Mother Teresa finally said in a letter to a spiritual advisor,

> For the first time in this 11 years I have come to love the darkness. For I believe now that it is a part, a very, very small part, of Jesus' darkness and pain on earth. You have taught me to accept it [as] a "spiritual side of 'your work,'" as you wrote. Today really I felt a deep joy that Jesus can't go anymore through agony but that He wants to go through it in me. More than ever I surrender myself to Him. Yes. More than ever, I will be at His disposal.[10]

Mother Teresa's crisis was so severe that many weaker Christians who faced it might have been destroyed by it. Without the clearly felt love and guidance of the Holy Spirit in their lives, they might have concluded that they were not really connected to God and that they should toss aside their faith as untrue. Mother Teresa's papers show that this loss of faith was a danger for her also. But instead, the crisis became a turning point that pushed her the other way, toward a more profound spiritual experience and ministry than would not have been possible otherwise. Despite her deep pain, by all accounts she radiated joy and balance and beautifully touched the lives of untold thousands of people for Jesus.

Kolodiejchuk wrote,

> Mother Teresa had reached the point in her life when she no longer ventured to penetrate or question the mystery of her unremitting darkness. She accepted it, as she did everything else that God willed or permitted, "with a big smile." . . . Aspiring to be completely at God's disposal, she marveled at His humility in using her "nothingness." Her very poverty was her meeting place with God. She was convinced that He used it in order to reach others.[11]

Mother Teresa's story is a powerful example of the cycle of doubt and belief in the Christian life, and the tipping points that may move a person from spiritual crisis to a deeper walk with God. Although her struggle was long-lasting and all encompassing, some crises of doubt creep up more slowly and do not present themselves in such a clear-cut way, as we'll explore in the next chapter.

Go to www.beaconhillbooks.com/go/godinpursuit for a free downloadable Study Guide that includes questions for deeper personal reflection as well as activities for use in a small-group setting.

ELEVEN

Where Doubt May Lead
A Small Complaint About Suffering

Mother Teresa's decades-long questioning of every aspect of her faith—from God's very existence to her own relationship with Him—was not an academic debate. It was not set off when she happened to be sitting around discussing the fine points of theology with a group of friends or when someone casually suggested that she read a book on the topic. Instead, she was forced to confront her doubt, agonize in prayer, and seek years of counsel from her spiritual advisors, because the deep personal pain of losing her sense of Jesus' presence left her with no other option.

Her anguish and confusion might have destroyed her faith, but it didn't. Instead, she learned to see her faith in a new way and to better understand how Jesus worked through her. In one sense it's possible to summarize her dilemma in a simple question: Why did Jesus withdraw the comforting, life-giving sense of His Spirit from her life?

She reached a tipping point into deeper faith when she came to believe an answer that also can be stated simply: The darkness she experienced was a way she could more fully take part in the pain that Jesus suffered on earth and a way she could more fully identify with the rejected, unwanted, hurting people she served.

Is that answer profound, or is it simplistic? It took Mother Teresa decades to arrive at it. What if someone had given her that answer at the beginning of her struggle? Would it have satisfied her? She could have understood it intellectually, but would it have penetrated deep within her?

In this chapter I want to focus not so much on the *issues* that raise doubts in the Christian life but rather on the *process* of how those doubts may creep in and how Christians really deal with them. In books on apologetics or in issue-oriented books, the questions are formulated in a formal, succinct way that can be answered with cleverly argued responses. In life, doubts often arrive in a messier fashion. The creeping doubt slinks in and threatens to undermine my faith even before I'm aware that I have any doubt. How much easier it would be if the doubt arrived by clearly announcing itself so that I could immediately engage it by consulting the relevant philosophers and scriptures.

Sometimes the issue is not even a doubt per se but more of a *complaint*. It may be something I believe, but it threatens to disrupt my faith because I find it so disturbing. It may be that God has made the world in a certain way, and I wish He hadn't. The complaint seeps in, it lingers, and if I don't find a way to come to terms with it, it may eat away at my relationship with Christ.

The issue I'll use as an example is suffering. Like Mother Teresa's dilemma, there's a fine line between profound answers to this issue and simplistic ones. When I've talked to Christians who are *not* struggling with suffering, it's easy for them to dismiss the whole problem with a statement such as "Oh, suffering is the result of the fallen state of humanity and the free will God has given us, so we just have to live with it" or "Suffering is hard, but God uses it to make us stronger."

Strangely, even those who grapple with the issue for years and read and think and pray and suffer often come to very similar conclusions, but for the first group it's a dismissive answer, and for the other group it's a deep insight filled with penetrating significance.

It's like many other big statements. Take "God loves you." That could be nothing more than a sappy platitude, but you may also reach a point when you *know* this to be true—and when the joy and amazement of this simple statement changes everything about how you see your life.

Creeping Doubt: The Example of Suffering

Not every crisis of doubt is as high-stakes or as long-lasting as the one that encompassed Mother Teresa. Some crises of creeping doubt and complaint operate at a more subtle level, gnawing at faith without drawing enough attention to itself to demand that the believer stop and find an answer immediately. When philosophers and scholars write about suffering, they often deal with it at the extremes. How could God allow the horrors of war and starvation and cruelty and sickness and injustice that plague the world every day? For some who examine suffering in this sweeping way, the issue can be a tipping point that turns them away from God.

Bart Ehrman, for instance, in his book *God's Problem: How the Bible Fails to Answer Our Most Important Question—Why We Suffer* comes to the conclusion that Christianity fails to provide a plausible response to this disturbing dilemma. He once was a Christian but now considers himself an agnostic.

Suffering—like other issues that provoke doubt or complaint— may not enter the individual Christian's spiritual life all at once as a grandiose debate about Holocausts and plagues but may instead arise more sporadically over the years at a far more personal level. At one point in a Christian's life, suffering may seem like such an abstract issue that one of the simple traditional answers to it will suffice. At other times the issue may seem so huge that the Christian avoids it because it seems beyond his or her capacity to probe. Sometimes a personal episode of horrible, life-altering suffering will bring the issue so much to the forefront of life that the Christian must find an answer now in order to continue being a follower of Christ.

And then there's the episode of suffering that I'm describing that's different from all those. For me, when the issue arrived in my life this time, it crept in as a painful, nagging complaint about the way God has set up the world. I say "this time," because it's not the first time I've confronted the issue, and I'm sure it won't be the last. I know that the answer I needed was provisional. In other words, I was not raising every possible theoretical conundrum that has ever been debated about this issue, so whatever answer I found would not solve every problem about this subject.

That's part of the messiness of doubt during the Christian life. The tipping point is reached when I have enough of an answer that I can—or cannot—continue with my faith, which may now have stretched and matured beyond anything I expected.

Having to "Face" Suffering

My recent skirmish with cancer was the triggering episode that brought the larger issue of suffering to the forefront of my thinking for a time and made me have to either squelch it, deny it, ignore it, or deal with it. As an example of suffering in itself, it wasn't much compared to what I know others are going through. It wasn't life-threatening, and it was treatable. But it was very visible and hard to ignore. I wore it right there on my face as a reminder to myself and everyone who saw me that bad, unexpected, ugly things happen that cause pain and serve no apparent purpose.

I had skin cancer, which I've battled repeatedly for the last ten years. This type was not the most dangerous kind I've had, but I had four separate areas of it on my face at the same time—two on my forehead, one on my left cheek, and worst of all, one on my nose that required a skin graft to cover the wound. Each area required a huge gash—or at least it seemed huge to me—to be gouged into my face, with ugly bandages covering the resulting swelling, scabs, and scars. I walked through life like this, taught my classes like this, endured the stares, and answered the questions and smiled at the lame jokes about this—for weeks.

Why? How does it help anybody for me to look like this or for my forehead to ache like this? If God loves me, why couldn't He have simply taken this away? Do I even have the right to ask that question knowing that my suffering is so small compared to what others are enduring? But the fact that others are worse off didn't change my dilemma. I didn't want them to suffer either. I was disgusted with the whole system.

Sensitized by my own sliced-up face to the problem of suffering, I began to see it everywhere within the next few weeks. Someone I love was diagnosed with a much worse form of cancer, and I was awash in dread for what she would have to endure. I felt the stab of fear, the "what if's" of where this would lead. Then I heard a prayer request at church for another person with cancer, then another, then one more.

People close to me endured other debilitating health setbacks. A close family member died. Friends had a financial meltdown and lost their home. On the television news the reporters told—almost casually, in that chipper news anchor tone—of the death of hundreds in the latest Middle East battle. Thousands more were killed in a conflict in Africa that I barely knew was happening. In a town near where I live, a man murdered an entire family.

This was not to mention all the much smaller examples of suffering that form the background of life—people with broken bones, colds, anxieties, sore throats, back pain, hearing loss; people suffering rejection, humiliation, insult, rude behavior from store clerks, bad tempers on the road, bullying, backstabbing. For what purpose?

During my own post-surgical, bandaged-faced, swollen-head period of perplexity about this issue, the *pointlessness* of the suffering, large or small, is what bothered me most. I thought, *If only I*

*didn't have this painful disruption of life to deal with, I could soar!
I could fly through life unbothered, undistracted from the tasks at
hand. I could stop having to answer the question "What happened
to your face?" I could meet my classes and focus on the material
I'm teaching rather than on whether the students are staring at—
or diverting their faces from—my wounds.*

If God would simply heal me, I would praise Him for it and even
more vigorously pursue the calling into which I believe He has led
me. How much better a witness for the gospel I could be if I could go
around telling everyone, "I thought I had skin cancer all over my face
and would need multiple surgeries and a skin graft to remove it, but
then I woke up one morning—and God had healed me!"

Why not? What would it cost Him? And why couldn't He do the
same for my relatives who were suffering and for many others? If
we absolutely *have* to have suffering, for heaven's sake, couldn't we
at least confine it to those who clearly have done something outrageous enough to deserve it—child-killers and rapists and people
like that? But for the rest of us, why not let us off the hook so we
can live with unimpeded joy?

I hate all the *waste.* I know intelligent, strong, talented people
who are eager to work but can't find jobs. I see them broke, in debt,
angry, frustrated, scared. For what purpose? All around me are
people who want to walk and run unimpeded but are hobbled by
old age, disease, and injury. An old couple I know totter across the
parking lot at church, holding each other up. Adventurous souls—
their pasts filled with boldness and daring—how they would love to
be limber and to scoop up the children and spin them around! How
they would love to have their hearing restored and read without a
magnifying glass and have their hands stop shaking and be beautiful again and clearheaded and clear-skinned and know every aspect
of life to its fullest. Instead, they suffer. Making it into the sanctuary will exhaust them for the day. What purpose is served by their
frustration and pain?

Things Fall Apart

I pondered these thoughts on the run. At this point I would not have called what I was going through a crisis of faith. I was searching for an answer, but not in any methodical way. If this were a more logical process, maybe I would have stopped at this point and "looked up the answer" for why God allows suffering. There are plenty of answers out there—hundreds of books on the topic, written by brilliant people. I came into this predicament having read some of them myself and having heard some of the other arguments secondhand in sermons and class discussions and informal conversations. In the back of my mind were some things I had read by Philip Yancey, C. S. Lewis, Timothy Keller, Dinesh D'Souza, and others. I had heard of Gottfried Liebniz's idea of God having created "the best of all possible worlds." I had heard arguments about how the free will God gave to humans led to the contamination of the world once humans abused that freedom by choosing evil. I had heard other arguments about the "soul-building" purposes of suffering and the ways it can bring people together.

At certain points in my Christian walk, these and other intellectual responses were all I needed. But now, my mind didn't move in those directions. Instead, I wanted an answer that not only satisfied my intellect but also reached down to my deepest levels of intuition and conviction. I wanted an answer so clear that I could respond, "Of course! *Now* I see it! It *has* to be this way! How could I have missed it?" I wanted to move forward so confidently that it transformed the way I thought about suffering and removed it—even if the suffering itself remained—as an issue of doubt and confusion and despair. Intellectual cleverness alone wouldn't get me there. I needed an answer more vital, more visceral and inevitable.

As I went about my business, a series of seemingly unrelated events happened, but somehow all of them got sucked into the vortex of my crisis of doubt and complaint. What happened was, everything started falling apart. I don't mean "falling apart" metaphorically. I mean that things around me literally crumbled or stopped working. Our washing machine broke down. My car was recalled for a minor problem, but when I got it to the dealer, he found a few thousand dollars of other repairs that needed to be done. A windstorm pushed two of the young trees in my yard to a precarious angle so that I had to stake them to keep them from falling over. As I put my eyeglasses on my face, I heard the wire frame crack, and a lens plopped into the sink. Why was everything disintegrating?

Then a small earthquake shook my house. My home is in southern California, a place where building a house at all means you're in denial of the fact that your home and all your earthly possessions could be shattered to pieces at any moment. The news was filled with geologists giving dire predictions of the faults all around me that are decades overdue for catastrophic quakes. One source kindly informed me that the ground on which I live rests on two tectonic plates—the North American and Pacific plates—that never stop grinding together.

Disintegration was all around, even in the smallest things. My favorite recliner, the best resting spot in my house for more than twenty years, collapsed and had to be thrown away. Part of the sprinkler system in my backyard quit working. A magazine article informed me that in the United States a person dies every twelve seconds.

Tipping Point: The Puff of Air

I continued to have the little surgeries on my face, one after another, and I contemplated the suffering of people I love, and I pondered the things falling apart all around me. As I grappled with these problems, one night I pulled out a thick file of notes I used for a talk I gave a few years earlier on the role of literature during hard times. In preparation for that speech, I had collected several months' worth of newspaper and magazine articles on disasters around the world. I went through these articles again. A tsunami in

Indonesia killed 285,000 people. I let myself think about that statistic alone for a while and was staggered. It's too many people to easily imagine. I tried to picture them in one place, but where? What room, building, or stadium would be big enough? In my mind I lined them up on a very long road, an avenue of relentless suffering.

I kept reading: stories of tens of thousands of people killed in earthquakes in Iran and Pakistan, a thick collection of articles on Hurricane Katrina. Beyond the human tragedy of that disaster—people killed, people made homeless, people who were jobless and frustrated and angry—one other statistic buried in one of the stories rose to my attention. Not many days after the Hurricane Katrina disaster, an expert estimated that before New Orleans could be rebuilt, twenty-two million tons of debris would have to be cleared away. Twenty-two million tons. That was only New Orleans and didn't take into consideration all the other areas of the Gulf Coast that were devastated by the hurricane.

Normally a statistic like that would float right past me, but I couldn't get it out of my head. What would twenty-two million tons of debris look like? I tried to think smaller and work up to it. What about one ton of debris? How much space would that take up in my room? How about ten tons? A thousand tons? One hundred thousand tons? My ability to comprehend this pile of garbage ran out long before I got to twenty-two million tons. Disintegration. Collapse. Everything falling apart.

For me, this heightened awareness that everything is falling apart, including my own sad face, was the tipping point toward coming to terms with this particular crisis of complaint over suffering.

Tucked into this file of disasters—though I hadn't actually used them in my talk—I found scriptures I had copied down dealing with the fleeting nature of human existence. Here was Eugene Peterson's version of Psalm 39:5-6—"Oh! We're all puffs of air. Oh! We're all shadows in a campfire! Oh! We're just spit in the wind. We make our pile, and then we leave it" (TM). I found my own summaries of Job 7 and Job 14, and when I looked them up again, I read verses like "Remember, O God, that my life is but a breath" (Job 7:7), and "Man born of woman is of few days and full of trouble. He springs up like a flower and withers away; like a fleeting shadow, he does not endure" (Job 14:1-2).

These words from Scripture led my mind to more familiar ones that I already carried around in my head but that now struck me in a new way. In Matthew 6 Jesus reminds me that nothing around me will last, so I shouldn't invest too much importance in all the temporary values that can be destroyed by hurricanes and tsunamis and age and a bad economy: "Do not store up for yourselves treasures on earth, where moth and rust destroy, and where thieves break in and steal" (Matthew 6:19).

All the suffering, all the disintegration in me and around me is a reminder that I'm part of something *eternal*. What's in front of me is fading away. In good times it looks and feels permanent. I keep forgetting it won't last forever. I keep thinking that if only I could get Now taken care of—the Now of my health, my standing in the world, my finances, my looks—then I would be content. But the suffering jolts me out of this dangerous complacency and urges me, *No, don't sink your trust into these things. They may look solid, but they'll soon be gone.* "But store up for yourselves treasures in heaven, where moth and rust do not destroy, and where thieves do not break in and steal" (Matthew 6:20).

I normally think of myself as optimistic. I try to make the best of things, not complain too much, focus on the good things of life. So all this emphasis on things falling apart and suffering and the shortness of life does not come natural to me. It feels too negative. I usually like to think of suffering and collapse as the exception to the rule, and I do everything I can to rush through it and get everything back to a more "permanent" state of order and normalcy. I see now that striving to find a permanent solution to these difficulties is not optimism but illusion. There's no permanent solution in this temporary place.

Around this time I found some amazing old photographs on a web site someone recommended called shorpy.com. It has hundreds of high-definition photographs going back to the 1850s. I don't know how they do it technologically, but these are the clearest and most vivid photos from those early times that I've ever seen. When I let one of those photos fill my whole computer screen, these faces from a hundred years ago or more look so real, so Now, that I feel as if I could easily step into their world or they could walk into mine.

One photo that caught my attention was a 1912 picture of five children of the Argentinian ambassador posed together in front of the steps of a mansion in Washington, D.C. None of them is smiling. All of them stare directly at the camera with varying degrees of consternation, eyebrows furrowed, as if they fear the photographer will keep them standing there all day. A boy about five or six years old sits in a metal toy car and looks as if he's eager to pedal away, as his toddler sister looks poised to follow him with her toy baby carriage. Two teenage girls in ugly matching dresses and wide-brimmed hats stand stiffly with pained expressions in the back row, while the brother in the center of the group tilts his head and frowns in annoyance as if he's about to jump forward and show the photographer how to work the camera so they can get this over with.

Except for the clothes, these could be the same impatient children that fill my house every day—my kids and their friends—playing basketball and video games and slamming the doors too hard and spilling food on the floor and having no real idea that they won't be like this forever. I looked at that photograph, so clear that it could have been taken only moments ago, and I couldn't help but think that all those kids must be dead by now, even the youngest girl. I see them in a moment when they thought time must be dragging on interminably. Little could they have dreamed that by the time I saw them nearly a hundred years later, peering at their faces on a device they could not have imagined, they would have lived their lives, grown old, deteriorated, and died. And those funny clothes gone too, and the toys, and probably even the building behind them demolished—fleeting.

Far from being pessimistic, these thoughts were strangely freeing. I could still enjoy my life, savor every moment, work and love and play, but I no longer felt the same pressure to make it all work out right. I'm a temporary resident, preparing for eternity, and no catastrophe can shake me from God's plan. I'm His child, so I can enjoy one of the greatest benefits of childhood—I can let someone else be in control.

As these days continued, circumstances led me to have to study Philippians, and I found myself newly drawn to the apostle Paul. This man, enduring the indignities of prison, writes to the Philippians without complaining about his suffering. He lives in such a vivid sense of the temporariness of the life that surrounds him and of the importance of the eternal implications of what he's doing that he sees his suffering as furthering his cause. He writes,

> Now I want you to know, brothers, that what has happened to me has really served to advance the gospel. As a result, it has become clear throughout the whole palace guard and to everyone else that I am in chains for Christ. Because of my chains, most of the brothers in the Lord have been encouraged to speak the word of God more courageously and fearlessly (Philippians 1:12-14).

Paul is so caught up in the eternal dimension of his life that he not only feels no need to fret over his own suffering, but even the question of whether he lives or dies is not a matter of much urgency to him:

> For to me, to live is Christ and to die is gain. If I am to go on living in the body, this will mean fruitful labor for me. Yet what shall I choose? I do not know! I am torn between the two: I desire to depart and be with Christ, which is better by far; but

it is more necessary for you that I remain in the body (Philippians 1:21-24).

Paul doesn't diminish the importance of the work he has to do here, but his awareness is never far from the next world, and that helps him not take the setbacks here too seriously. Later in that letter he says that he has "learned to be content whatever the circumstances. I know what it is to be in need, and I know what it is to have plenty. I have learned the secret of being content in any and every situation, whether well fed or hungry, whether living in plenty or in want. I can do everything through him who gives me strength" (Philippians 4:11-13).

I had read those verses many times, but now I wondered, as if reading them for the first time, is it really possible to find that level of contentment in the midst of suffering? If the veil between you and eternity is really so thin, then would a situation that would otherwise be considered a catastrophe now look like a temporary nuisance on the road to a far greater place?

I had nowhere near Paul's ability to live in such a constant awareness of eternity, but my perspective began to change at least to this extent: some things that once seemed crucial, or worth stewing over, or worth fighting for, started to fade in significance. An argument at work, the insult someone delivered at church, my worry over what people would think about how beaten-up my face looked—these and a dozen other worries assumed a lesser place.

As these thoughts took hold, I found myself spending less time striving to force certain outcomes in my life and more time appreciating the joys life offers even in the midst of suffering. It's similar to what happens to me at times on the racquetball court, when I'm so intent on winning that the game takes on a significance in my mind far beyond its real importance. I reach a point of intensity when I would give almost anything to win, but once it's over, win or lose, I walk off the court with my friend, and the game fades into oblivion like melting snow. None of this scurrying around and plotting and straining can make me or save me. I can set it all aside for a while and celebrate the Lord, thanking Him for letting me live this amazing life, even with its temporary troubles.

Beyond the Tipping Point: More Surprises

When first diagnosed with the cancer that would kill him, former White House Press Secretary Tony Snow wrote that the natural first response was to turn to God as a "cosmic Santa" to make it all go away. But then, Snow said, "another voice whispers: 'You have been called.' Your quandary has drawn you closer to God, closer to those you love, closer to the issues that matter—and has dragged into insignificance the banal concerns that occupy our 'normal time.'" Snow also wrote of another unexpected response, "an inexplicable shudder of excitement, as if a clarifying moment of calamity has swept away everything trivial and tinny, and placed before us the challenge of important questions."[1]

Up to now I thought suffering was the greatest thing to fear, and the trick was to try to live carefully enough to avoid it for as long as possible. Now I see I'm probably in even more spiritual danger during the good times than the bad. When I rack up an accomplishment, acquire a big possession, get everything I want, how easy it is to think, "This is what I deserve. These are the things that are important." I grow defensive against anyone or anything that might challenge my rightful position. I live in privilege, but since the foundation is the sand of a fleeting world that is passing away, I also live in unacknowledged fear of losing it. When suffering comes, I greet it as an outrage, a failure of God to preserve what is rightfully mine.

My new awareness of the fleeting nature of life, the futility of trying to put my trust in temporary values, the need to live with a sense of what matters for eternity—these factors were the tipping points in my own crisis of complaint. I know this doesn't answer every question about suffering. I reached a tipping point, not

150

a stopping point. Beyond the tipping point, even the smaller truths revealed themselves.

As the leaves of our giant tree in the backyard turned yellow and began to fall like a shower of confetti one afternoon, I joked with my kids that we were going to have to get rid of that tree because all the leaves were dying and dropping off. "What happened to it?" I complained. "The leaves used to be so green, but now look at all these dead leaves all over the yard. Who did this?"

But the kids know the tree is just fine. Death and destruction are built into nature, but so is resurrection. Before long we'll have even more green leaves on that tree than we did before, and it will grow higher than it's ever been.

All around us, resurrection. The seed gets buried in the ground, but the plant springs up. "For whoever wants to save his life will lose it, but whoever loses his life for me will save it," says Jesus. "What good is it for a man to gain the whole world, and yet lose or forfeit his very self?" (Luke 9:24-25).

Into suffering unexpected mercies are built. I used to think it strange when I would hear people who had suffered some catastrophe begin their story with a phrase like "We were just lucky" that this or that didn't happen. I would think, if you were *really* lucky, *none* of this would have happened. Still, I know what they're talking about. In the midst of disaster, when you're startled into considering all you could have lost, it makes you even more grateful for what you still have.

During good times I easily give no thought to all that has already been provided—my ability to breathe, my food, my ability to walk and run, my job, my relationships with my wife and children, my relationships with close friends, and my ability to see, hear, think, and read. These and a thousand other gifts I simply expect to be there as part of the package that is my life. But when one of the big ones is threatened, I wake up to the value of all the others. I see that I live a life suffused with good things, despite my setbacks.

I recently heard a prayer request from a woman who had multiple illnesses, lived alone with great difficulty, had very little money to live on, and was in debt. Plenty of problems, but the focus of her request was gratitude: she was thankful that someone had just dropped off food for her that would last for two weeks, thus allowing her to use some of her food money to meet a deadline for a loan payment. She was thrilled. In the meantime, I had just wolfed down a big meal with friends from work with barely a thought about how fortunate I was.

In the depths of suffering, a piercing sense of the presence of the Holy Spirit sometimes settles in on us, defying our circumstances. As Tony Snow wrote,

> When our faith flags, he throws reminders in our way. Think of the prayer warriors in our midst. . . . It is hard to describe, but there are times when suddenly the hairs on the back of your neck stand up, and you feel a surge of the Spirit. Somehow you just know: Others have chosen, when talking to the Author of all creation, to lift us up—to speak of us![2]

For at least a short time, we may feel overwhelmed with the knowledge that this is not all there is, that suffering is not the final word, that God is pursuing a purpose that is taking us somewhere better. Even though we may not be able to articulate any purpose for our suffering, we know God is with us in the midst of it.

Go to www.beaconhillbooks.com/go/godinpursuit for a free downloadable Study Guide that includes questions for deeper personal reflection as well as activities for use in a small-group setting.

Notes

Introduction

1. Francis S. Collins, *The Language of God: A Scientist Presents Evidence for Belief* (New York: Free Press, 2006), 7.

Chapter 1

1. Sara Miles, *Take This Bread: A Radical Conversion* (New York: Ballantine Books, 2008), xii-xiii, 7, 60.

2. Anne Lamott, *Traveling Mercies: Some Thoughts on Faith* (New York: Anchor Books, 1999), 9.

3. C. S. Lewis, *Surprised by Joy* (New York: Harcourt, Brace and World, 1955), 227.

4. Lamott, *Traveling Mercies*, 41.

5. Ibid., 49.

6. Miles, *Take This Bread*, 57-59.

7. Ziya Meral, "Bearing the Silence of God," *Christianity Today*, March 20, 2008, <http://www.christianitytoday.com/ct/2008/march/29.41.html>.

8. Will Vaus, "The Original Wiretapper," *The Los Angeles Times*, April 1, 2008, A15.

9. Will Vaus, *My Father Was a Gangster: The Jim Vaus Story* (Washington, D.C.: Believe Books, 2007), 70-71.

10. Ibid., 77.

11. Timothy Keller, *Prodigal God: Recovering the Heart of the Christian Faith* (New York: Dutton, 2008), xiv-xv.

12. Ibid., 27.

13. Ibid., 77.

Chapter 2

1. Jerome Murphy-O'Connor, *Paul: His Story* (Oxford, England: Oxford University Press, 2004), 24.

2. Richard V. Peace, *Conversion in the New Testament: Paul and the Twelve* (Grand Rapids: Wm. B. Eerdmans, 1999), 25-26.

3. Ibid., 54.

4. Lauren F. Winner, *Girl Meets God: On the Path to a Spiritual Life* (Chapel Hill, N.C.: Algonquin Books of Chapel Hill, 2002), 7-8.

5. Ibid., 57.

6. Ibid., 55-56.

7. Ibid., 57.

8. Udo Schnelle, *Apostle Paul: His Life and Theology*, trans. M. Eugene Boring (Grand Rapids.: Baker Academic, 2003), 81.

9. Murphy-O'Connor, *Paul: His Story*, 5.

10. Schnelle, *Apostle Paul*, 70-75.

11. Lamott, *Traveling Mercies*, 3.

12. Miles, *Take This Bread*, 23.

13. Vaus, "The Original Wiretapper," A15.

14. Dale L. Sullivan, "Kairos and the Rhetoric of Belief," *The Quarterly Journal of Speech* 78, no. 3 (August 1992): 321.

15. Frederick Buechner, quoted in Chad Wriglesworth, "George A. Buttrick and Frederick Buechner: Messengers of Reconciling Laughter," *Christianity and Literature* 53, no. 1 (August 2003): 64.

16. Frederick Buechner, *The Sacred Journey* (New York: Walker and Company, 1984), 162.

17. Hugh T. Kerr and John M. Mulder, ed., *Famous Conversions* (Grand Rapids: Wm. B. Eerdmans, 1999), 129.

18. Charles H. Spurgeon, *The Autobiography of Charles H. Spurgeon: Complied from His Diary, Letters, and Records by His Wife and His Private Secretary, Volume I* (Chicago: Curts & Jennings, 1898), 102.

19. Ibid.

20. Ibid., 105.

21. Ibid., 106.

Chapter 3

1. Malcolm Muggeridge, *Conversion: The Spiritual Journey of a Twentieth-Century Pilgrim* (Eugene, Ore.: Wipf & Stock, 1988), 21.

2. Clare Booth Luce, quoted in John A. O'Brien, ed., *The Road to Damascus* (Garden City, N.Y.: Doubleday, 1949), 223.

3. Ibid., 224-25.

4. Lewis R. Rambo, *Understanding Religious Conversion* (New Haven, Conn.: Yale University Press, 1993), 165.

5. Gordon T. Smith, *Beginning Well: Christian Conversion and Authentic Transformation* (Downers Grove, Ill.: InterVarsity Press, 2001), 16.

6. Ibid., 138-41.

7. *Evangelical Dictionary of Theology*, 2nd ed., s.v. "conversion" (by D. G. Bloesch).

8. Campus Crusade for Christ International, "How to Know God Personally," <http://www.ccci.org/wij/index.aspx>.

9. James Choung, quoted in an interview with Andy Crouch, "From Four Laws to Four Circles," *Christianity Today*, July 2008, 31.

10. Tim Stafford, *Surprised by Jesus: His Agenda for Changing Everything in A.D. 30 and Today* (Downers Grove, Ill.: Intervarsity Press, 2006), 67, 72-73.

Chapter 4

1. Brian "Head" Welch, *Save Me From Myself,* (New York: Harper One, 2007), 2.

2. Joe Eszterhas, *Crossbearer: A Memoir of Faith*, (New York: St. Martin's Press, 2008), 4-5.

3. Welch, *Save Me From Myself*, 18.

4. Ibid., 124-27.

5. Eszterhas, *Crossbearer*, 5-7.

6. John Woolman, *The Journal of John Woolman and a Plea for the Poor* (New York: Corinth Books, 1961), 5.

7. Jeff Friend, "Healed by a Wound," *Light and Life*, July/August 2008, pull-out section.

8. John Newton, *The Works of the Rev. John Newton*, Vol. 1 (New Haven, Conn.: Nathan Whiting, 1828), 40-41.

9. Ibid., 64-65.

10. Smith, *Beginning Well*, 14.

Chapter 5

1. Linda Freeman, e-mail message to Author, April 2, 2008.

2. Myles Weiss, "Meeting My Matchmaker," *Light & Life*, November/December 2006, pullout section.

3. Mary Adele LaClair, e-mail message to Author, May, 2009.

4. Thomas Allbaugh, e-mail message to Author, July 1, 2008.

5. E. Stanley Jones, *A Song of Ascents: A Spiritual Autobiography* (Nashville: Abingdon Press, 1968), 26-27.

6. Ibid., 27-28.

7. Newton, *The Works of the Rev. John Newton*, 65.

Chapter 6

1. Peter Cartwright, *Autobiography of Peter Cartwright* (Nashville: Abingdon Press, 1984), 36-37.

2. Ibid., 37-38.

3. C. S. Lewis, *Mere Christianity* (San Francisco: Harper San Francisco, 2001), 55-56.

4. *Evangelical Dictionary of Theology*, 2nd ed., s.v. "salvation" (by R. E. O. White).

5. Richard V. Peace, *Conversion in the New Testament: Paul and the Twelve* (Grand Rapids: Eerdmans, 1999), 28-29.

6. David Brainerd, quoted in Kerr and Mulder, *Famous Conversions*, 74.

7. Ibid.

8. Ibid., 79

9. Charles W. Colson, *Born Again* (Old Tappan, N.J.: Chosen Books, 1976), 110.

10. Ibid., 113-17.

11. Ibid., 130.

12. Basyle and Aram Tchividjian, *Invitation: Billy Graham and the Lives God Touched* (Colorado Springs: Multnomah Press, 2008), 47.

13. Ibid., 100.

Chapter 7

1. Jodi Werhanowicz, *Rogue Angel* (Phoenix: Ezekiel Press, 2005), 65, 87-88, 128.

2. Ibid., 109.

3. Ibid., 112-13.

4. Augustine, quoted in Kerr and Mulder, *Famous Conversions*, 12-13.

5. Jonathan Edwards, quoted in Ibid., 68.

6. Charles G. Finney, *Memoirs of Rev. Charles G. Finney* (New York: A. S. Barnes & Company, 1876), 16-17.

7. Eugenia Price and Faith Coxe Bailey, *Unshackled: Stories of Transformed Lives* (Chicago: Moody Press, 1952), 11-13.

8. Werhanowicz, *Rogue Angel*, iii.

Chapter 8

1. Francis S. Collins, *The Language of God: A Scientist Presents Evidence for Belief* (New York: Free Press, 2006), 16.

2. C. S. Lewis, *Surprised by Joy: The Shape of My Early Life* (New York: Harcourt, Brace and Co., 1955), 58, 66, 60.

3. Collins, *The Language of God*, 20.

4. Ibid., 29-30.

5. Ibid., 220, 223, 225.

6. Ibid., 5-6.

7. Lewis, *Surprised by Joy*, 172, 191, 213.

8. Ibid., 216, 223-24, 228-29.

9. Ibid., 235-237.

10. Muggeridge, *Conversion*, 14.

11. Ibid., 104-105.

12. Ibid., 110, 111, 133.

Chapter 9

1. John Wesley, *The Journal of John Wesley*, ed. Nehemiah Curnock (New York: Capricorn Books, 1963), 51-52.

2. John Bunyan, quoted in Kerr and Mulder, *Famous Conversions*, 50-51.

3. Wesley, *Journal*, 51-52.

4. Bunyan, *Famous Conversions*, 52.

5. Wesley, *Journal*, 52.

6. William James, *The Varieties of Religious Experience: A Study in Human Nature* (Scotts Valley, Calif.: IAP), 126-27.

7. Charles G. Finney, *Memoirs of Rev. Charles G. Finney*, 20-23.

8. Albert Schweitzer, quoted in Kerr and Mulder, *Famous Conversions*, 191-193.

9. Sara Miles, quoted in *Religion & Ethics Newsweekly* profile, PBS, May 25, 2007, <http://www.pbs.org/wnet/religionandethics/week1039/p-profile.html>.

10. C. F. Andrews, quoted in Kerr and Mulder, *Famous Conversions*, 176.

11. Peace, *Conversion in the New Testament*, 93.

Chapter 10

1. Scot McKnight and Hauna Ondrey, *Finding Faith, Losing Faith: Stories of Conversion and Apostasy* (Waco, Tex.: Baylor University Press, 2008), 49-50.

2. Julia Duin, *Quitting Church: Why the Faithful Are Fleeing and What to Do About It* (Grand Rapids: Baker Books, 2008), 22.

3. Timothy Keller, *The Reason for God: Belief in an Age of Skepticism* (New York: Dutton, 2008), xvi.

4. Barbara Brown Taylor, *Leaving Church: A Memoir of Faith* (New York: Harper One, 2007), xiii.

5. Mother Teresa, *Come Be My Light: The Private Writings of the "Saint of Calcutta,"* ed. Brian Kolodiejchuk (New York: Doubleday, 2007), 28, 154.

6. Ibid., 210.

7. Ibid., 3.

8. Ibid., 187.

9. Ibid., 216.

10. Ibid., 214.

11. Ibid., 272-73.

Chapter 11

1. Tony Snow, "Cancer's Unexpected Blessings," *Christianity Today*, July 14, 2008, <http://www.christianitytoday.com/ct/article_print.html?id=47315>.

2. Ibid.

Acknowledgments

I am grateful to many friends, family members, and colleagues for their help and encouragement as I wrote this book.

I am thankful to everyone at Beacon Hill Press of Kansas City who believed in this book and helped make it possible. Bonnie Perry has been a steady source of encouragement, Barry Russell has been constantly helpful, and Judi Perry is an excellent editor.

I am grateful to Shannon Selander, my departmental assistant in the English Department at Azusa Pacific University, who helped track down sources and assisted me in many other ways. Mary Adele LaClair was very helpful in reading a large portion of one of my later drafts of the book and suggesting changes.

One of my biggest sources of support for writing has been The Niños, a group of Christian writers and artists to which I belong. They prayed for this book from the early idea stage to its completion. In particular, I would especially like to thank Tom Allbaugh, Diana Glyer, Mike Glyer, Lynn Maudlin, Elena Smith, John Barnts, Lois Carlson, Tim and Teresa Davis, Kayla Winiarz, Monica Ganas, and Liz Leahy.

Steve Laube is my superb agent, and I am grateful for all the help he has given me.

I wish to thank my colleagues at Azusa Pacific University for all they have done to make this book and my other writing possible. Provost Michael Whyte has been a continuing source of encouragement. My colleagues in the English Department have created an atmosphere of friendship and productivity that inspires me to keep writing. Special thanks go to David Esselstrom, David Weeks, and Diane Guido.

The Spectrum Class at Glendora (California) Community Church allowed me to try out some of the ideas in this book on them as I was writing it. I appreciate their help and prayers. I am also thankful for our Pastor, Mike Platter, whose messages have challenged and inspired me.

Without the support of my family, writing this or any other book would not be possible. I am grateful for the love of my parents and my sister Debbie. I also am particularly thankful for the love, support, and patience of my wife, Peggy, and my children, Jacob and Katie.

About the Author

Joseph Bentz is the author of *When God Takes Too Long*, *Silent God*, and four novels. He is professor of English at Azusa Pacific University, in Azusa, California, where he teaches courses in writing and American literature. He earned Ph.D. and M.A. degrees in American literature from Purdue University and a B.A. degree in English from Olivet Nazarene University. He lives with his wife and two children in southern California. More information about his books and speaking can be found at <www.josephbentz.com>.

For more information or to contact the author, visit
<www.josephbentz.com>.